THE LOWFAT JEWISH VEGETARIAN COOKBOOK

ALSO BY DEBRA WASSERMAN

Simply Vegan
(With Reed Mangels, Ph.D.,R.D.)

Meatless Meals for Working People
(With Charles Stahler)

No Cholesterol Passover Recipes
(With Charles Stahler)

This book is dedicated to my grandmother, Mollie Weintraub, who in her nineties still enjoys life's simple pleasure of sitting down to a delicious meal with her grandaughter. This woman is truly an inspiration to me.

THE LOWFAT JEWISH VEGETARIAN COOKBOOK

Healthy Traditions From Around The World

By Debra Wasserman

The Vegetarian Resource Group
Baltimore, Maryland

A NOTE TO THE READER

The contents of *The Lowfat Jewish Vegetarian Cookbook* are not intended to provide personal medical advice. Medical advice should be obtained from a qualified health professional.

© Copyright 1994, Debra Wasserman
Published by The Vegetarian Resource Group,
PO Box 1463, Baltimore, Maryland 21203.

Library of Congress Cataloging-in-Publication Data
The Lowfat Jewish Vegetarian Cookbook -- Healthy
Traditions From Around The World/Debra Wasserman
Library of Congress Catalog Card Number: 93-61354

ISBN 0-931411-12-2

Printed in the United States of America
10 9 8 7 6 5 4 3 2

CONTENTS

FOREWORD

In the summer of 1978, I was fortunate to have the opportunity to study in Israel for six weeks. It was only then that I truly learned how diverse Jewish lifestyles and customs are throughout the world. Having been raised on Long Island, New York, I had come to believe that all Jews ate the same type of bagels, knishes, and kugel puddings as my family did. Most of the Jewish people I knew were of Russian or European descent. My own relatives came from Poland, Russia, and Austria.

While traveling throughout Israel and doing research at Hebrew University in Jerusalem, I met Jews from many different countries. Whether they came from Ireland, Morocco, Yemen, South Africa, or Brazil, each had their own favorite dish and stories to share. I remember being fascinated with this information.

According to the book, *Jewish Cooking From Around The World*, by Josephine Levy Bacon, the first American Jewish cookbook was called *The Jewish Cookery Book*. It was written by Mrs. Esther Levy nee Jacobs in 1871 and published in Philadelphia. Since then hundreds of Jewish cookbooks have been printed.

Two and one half years ago, I was thumbing through some of these Jewish cookbooks and couldn't help but notice all the emphasis put on meat-based meals. Most of the recipes I reviewed were high in fat and cholesterol. Vegetables were usually categorized as side dishes and then were often laden with extra fat, too.

In *The International Jewish Encyclopedia* it is stated that, "Jewish law strictly enjoins man to preserve and take care of his health -- man must do anything in his power to preserve his life, and not commit any act which might be injurious to his physical well-being." Nevertheless, many Jewish cookbooks offer high-fat recipes that promote sickness, rather than health.

Today, most Rabbis speak out against smoking. Even some Yeshivas have banned smoking in their buildings. And yet, when it comes to the type of food Jews eat each day, not enough commentary is heard.

With these thoughts in mind, I decided to spend a great deal of time the past two years researching and writing this cookbook. It was not a simple task. I did a lot of reading. However, food choices beyond the issue of what is and what isn't kosher are not discussed often in Jewish history books. Next, I spent time speaking to Jews from different countries.

What I learned is that Jews from around the world traditionally have eaten healthy vegetarian meals. Until now no American Jewish cookbook has focused on these wonderful dishes. It is my hope that you will enjoy the recipes in this lowfat international Jewish cookbook and share them with your family and friends.

-- Debra Wasserman

ACKNOWLEDGEMENTS

I would like to thank Reed Mangels, Ph.D., R.D., for doing the nutritional analysis for each recipe and offering me valuable suggestions, and Mary Clifford, R.D. and Charles Stahler for writing the section titled *Figuring Fat*. Thank you also to Mircea Stoiadin who shared his traditional Romanian recipes with me and Ruth Stahler for developing some of the recipes found in this book. Thanks to Amy Greenebaum and Carole Hamlin for proof-reading the manuscript and to the staff and volunteers at The Vegetarian Resource Group for tasting many of the recipes and giving me constructive feed-back.

I also appreciate all the kind assistance I received from the enthusiastic and hardworking staffs of Baltimore's Pratt Library and Peabody Library, Philadelphia's Public Library, and New York's Public Library. And finally, special thanks to Charles Stahler for the support I continue to receive each day and to my mother, Muriel Wasserman, for sharing her wonderful cooking, artistry, and creative talents with me.

GLOSSARY

Throughout this cookbook there may be some ingredients or words that are unfamiliar to the reader. With this in mind, here is a glossary of less familiar terms for your assistance.

Baba Ganouj is a Middle Eastern dish consisting of puréed baked eggplant, tahini, and spices. It is usually served as an appetizer or spread along with pita bread.

Bagels are made out of yeast dough twisted into a doughnut-like shape that is first boiled in water then baked in an oven. They usually have a hard crust and may be sprinkled with different items such as sesame or poppy seeds, minced onion or garlic, etc.

Barley is a small white grain with a thin brown line running down the center which separates each grain into two sections. It takes about 1 hour and 15 minutes to cook barley in boiling water and it can be used in soups, puddings, or as a substitute for rice in dishes.

Basmati Rice is a popular variety of rice grown and used frequently in India. It is a long-grain rice and is white or brown.

Blackstrap Molasses is the lowest grade of molasses, which is the by-product of the manufacturing of sugar from sugar cane. Blackstrap molasses is dark brown in color and it is a sweetener.

Blini are Russian pancakes served as a main dish. They are made out of yeast-raised buckwheat flour batter.

Blintzes are filled thin pancakes made out of flour and stuffed with various items including fruit or potatoes.

Borscht is Russian beet soup that is served either hot or chilled.

Brown Rice is a whole grain where only the hull has been removed. It can be served alone or in soups, stews, puddings, etc.

Brown Rice Flour is made from brown rice and does not contain gluten. It is often used to make pancakes.

Buckwheat Flour is usually stoneground from unhulled buckwheat and is often used in pancakes.

Buckwheat Groats or Kasha are the kernels that remain after the removal of the hulls from buckwheat, which botanically is a fruit and a member of the grass family. It is used as a cereal or in stuffing, side and main dishes, etc.

Bulgur, also known as cracked wheat, is wheat that has been prepared for cooking or soaking and eating raw by cracking, steaming, and toasting. It can be eaten alone as a side dish, or used in puddings, soups, stews, stuffing, etc.

Challah is bread usually served at the Sabbath meal. Traditionally it contains eggs, but it can also be made eggless.

Charoset is a traditional Passover dish consisting of grated fruit (often apples), chopped nuts, wine, and cinnamon. There are many variations of this dish from different countries.

Chickpeas, also known as garbanzo beans and ceci beans, are primarily grown in Mediterranean countries. These off-white seeds are used fresh or dried in stews, spreads, soups, and side and main dishes. Dried chickpeas take several hours to cook from scratch in boiling water, but can also be bought pre-cooked in cans.

Chicory can be used as one of the five bitter herbs on the Passover Seder menu. It is a green or red leafy plant used in salads or sautéed into a side dish.

Cholent, also known as hamin, is a traditional slow-cooked, one-pot Sabbath dish. It usually contains beans, potatoes, barley, and other vegetables and/or fruit.

Cilantro is a fresh green herb that looks like parsley with a larger leaf. When dried it is known as coriander. Fresh it is also called Chinese parsley and is used in soups, stews, stuffing, salads, etc.

Cornmeal is ground white or yellow corn. It is used to bake breads or pancakes.

Couscous, which starts as durum wheat, originated in North Africa and can be milled to the degree of fineness preferred. It is not a whole grain, since 100 percent of its bran and germ are removed in processing. It is a very small round, off-white grain that cooks in minutes.

Curry is a popular Indian spice and also the name of Indian stews that contain curry.

Dates are the fruit of the date palm tree and when fresh have a yellow-red skin and a sweet, wine taste. They are also sold dried and can be eaten raw, used in puddings and salads, or cooked in stuffing and stews.

Falafel is an appetizer or sandwich filler served in pita bread with tahini sauce. It is round and made from cooked chickpeas.

Fava Beans, also known as broad beans, are available dried or fresh. They cook slowly in boiling water for about 1 hour and can be bought pre-cooked in cans. They have a flat kidney-shape and are green when fresh, buff when dried. In the Middle East they are often a substitute for chickpeas. Fava beans can be eaten as a side dish or spread, or in soups and casseroles.

Figs are fruit that grow on trees. There are many varieties, the four main types being green, white, purple, or red in color. Figs are often available fresh or dried. They are very sweet and can be used in stuffing, desserts, and cholent, or eaten alone.

Goulash is a stew traditionally made with meat, onions, vegetables, paprika, and other spices. It can be prepared with meat substitutes such as seitan.

Grape Leaves, also known as vine leaves, are usually found pickled in bottles or cans today. Sometimes they can be found fresh in ethnic/gourmet stores. They look like leaves and are used as wrappers for stuffing.

Hamentashen are traditional baked goods served during Purim. Traditionally, they are made out of flour and eggs and stuffed with fruit or poppy seed filling. They can be made eggless.

Horseradish is a perennial herb related to the mustard family. It is grown mainly for its roots, which are grated before being bottled. It is commonly used for one of the bitter herbs in the Passover Seder service and has a hot flavor.

Hummus is a spread made out of puréed chickpeas, tahini, and spices. It is often served with pita bread.

Kishke traditionally is matzo meal or bread crumbs, onions, etc. stuffed in a beef casing and then steamed and roasted. It can be made without the beef casing and served like stuffing.

Kneidlach are matzo balls traditionally made out of matzo meal (finely ground matzo) and eggs. They can be made eggless and served in vegetable broth.

Knish is a thin piece of rolled dough folded over a filling such as mashed potatoes, spinach, kasha and onions, etc. The dough often contains eggs, but can be made eggless.

Kohlrabi, also known as Hungarian turnip, is a root vegetable with blue-green leaves. An above-ground vegetable contains an edible flesh with a slight flavor of celery.

Kugel is a pudding usually made out of potatoes or noodles. Traditionally, it contains eggs, but can be made eggless.

Latkes are potato pancakes traditionally served during Chanukah. Often they also contain eggs, but they can be made eggless. Serve them with applesauce or other pureed cooked fruit.

Leek is a cultivated member of the lily family. They have long, flat, white and green leaves and look like an enormous scallion, to which it is related. They must be carefully rinsed before using in soups, salads, side dishes, etc, because dirt is caught in the leaves.

Lentils are legumes that originated in Asia. There are over sixty varieties that vary in color and size. In the United States small greenish brown lentils are most common. To a lesser extent red lentils are also found. Lentils cook in just under one hour in boiling water and are used in soups, spreads, croquettes, and side and main dishes.

Matzo is unleavened bread traditionally eaten during Passover. It is sometimes ground finely into matzo meal and matzo flour.

Millet is a grain that is mainly grown in warm climates. It cooks in 45 minutes or less in boiling water. Millet is small and round with an off-white appearance that can be used alone as a side dish or in soups, stews, pudding, or casseroles.

Okra pods look like little lime-green rockets and have a velvety feel. Inside are rows of tiny seeds in a slippery membrane sack. Okra is used in curry dishes and Mediterranean meals. Choose small okra (up to three inches long), since they taste best.

Phyllo Dough comes in very thin sheets made out of flour and is used as a wrapper to make pastries, turnovers, and other baked goods. It often is sold in freezer cases in supermarkets.

Pilaf, also known as pilav, is a spiced rice casserole. Sometimes other grains such as bulgur are substituted for the rice.

Pine Nuts, also known as pignoli, are nuts from pine trees. They are used in stuffing and desserts often with dried fruit.

Pita is a round flat bread made out of white or whole wheat flour. It is very popular in the Middle East and is now widely available in the United States.

Pomegranate, also known as Chinese Apple, grows both as a fruit tree and shrub. Pomegranate seeds are red in color and can be eaten raw in salads and desserts. They are sometimes pressed into a juice or dried and eaten like raisins.

Poppy Seeds are blue-gray seeds from the opium poppy plant. They are used in baking and in curry dishes.

Rhubarb is a plant with tuberous roots, thick juicy red stems, and large coarse inedible leaves. Rhubarb stalks are best when young and pink in color. Rhubarb is used in soups, stews, and pies.

Rye Flour is obtained by milling rye, a cereal crop. It is available in white, medium, and dark grades and is used in bread making, usually combined with wheat flour.

Seitan is made from wheat and is gluten cooked in soy sauce. To make seitan, water is added to wheat flour and then kneaded into a dough consistency. The bran and starch are then repeatedly rinsed out until only gluten remains. Seitan is a great meat substitute.

Soy Milk is milk made out of soybeans. It contains no cholesterol and some lowfat varieties are now available.

Split Peas are dried yellow or green peas. They take 1 hour to cook in boiling water and are used in soups, spreads, and stews.

Tabouli, also known as tabouleh, is a salad made from bulgur, vegetables, and fresh herbs.

Tahini is sesame seed butter made from ground hulled sesame seeds. It has a beige color and can be used in salad dressings, dips and spreads, gravies, soups, etc.

Tofu is a soybean curd product, whereby soybeans are soaked, ground, and filtered, with the remaining mixture heated and a coagulant added, which results in soy curd and whey. The soy curd is pressed to make hard or soft tofu, which is then used in soups, desserts, salads, dips and spreads, etc.

Turnips, similar to rutabagas, are quicker growing than other root vegetables. Turnip flesh is white and the tops are leafy green. Occasionally, rutabagas with yellow flesh are sold. Turnip leaves can be eaten as well, especially when seasoned. Turnips are used in cholent, stews, soups, etc.

Unbleached White Flour is not a whole grain flour. It is, however, ideal for imparting a lightness to baked goods and an environmental improvement over bleached white flour.

Varnishkes, also known as varnishkas, are noodles traditionally made out of flour and eggs. However, eggless noodles available on supermarket shelves today can be substituted.

Wheat Berries are whole grains of wheat that are cooked for two hours in boiling water and used in puddings, side and main dishes, etc. They can be used in place of rice or barley in some dishes.

Wheat Germ is the oil-containing portion of the wheat kernel. It is used to enrich breads, as a topping, cereal, etc.

Whole Wheat Pastry Flour is often not stoneground, but rather milled in a hammer mill that reduces the soft white or red wheat to small, uniform particles. It is used for baking pie crusts, cookies, and other baked goods.

MENUS

BREAKFAST IDEAS

Fresh Fruit
Banana Bagel (pg. 30) or Cake-Like Rye Bread (pg. 33)
   with Hummus (pg. 46)

Blueberry/Banana Matzo Meal Pancakes (pg. 32)
Juice

Baked Fruit (pg. 174)
Toasted Whole Grain Bread with Jam

Bulgur and Grape Salad (pg. 74)
Juice

Polish Apple Blintzes (pg. 37)
Juice

Rice Flour Pancakes (pg. 40)
Melon

LUNCH IDEAS AT HOME

Mixed Green Salad
Cream of Mushroom Soup (pg. 56)
Pita Bread (pg. 36) or Russian Flat Bread (pg. 41)

Moroccan Chickpea and Lentil Soup (pg. 59)
Potato Knish (pg. 156), Spinach knish (pg. 166),
    Sauerkraut Knish (pg. 165) or Kasha and Onions Knish
    (pg. 150)

Tossed Salad
Potato Latkes (pg. 159) or Broccoli Latkes (pg. 139)
Applesauce

Yemenite Green Bean Soup (pg. 72)
Stuffed Tomato (pg. 137) or Stuffed Mushrooms (pg. 136)

Mock Chopped "Liver" (pg. 49)
Eggless Challah (pg. 34)
Sliced Tomatoes and Cucumbers

Polish Mushroom Barley Soup (pg. 60)
Spinach Pie (pg. 119)

LUNCH IDEAS AWAY FROM HOME

Polish Dilled Cucumbers (pg. 81)
Pumpernickel Bread (pg. 38)
Mock Chopped "Liver" (pg. 49)

Leftover Chickpea Cutlets (pg. 93) served with
    ketchup or barbecue sauce
Leftover Salad

Israeli Stuffed Grape Leaves (pg. 130)
Hummus (pg. 46) or Baba Ghanoush (pg. 42)
Pita Bread (pg. 36)

Garden Salad
Russian Cold Borscht (pg. 65) or Cold Cherry Soup (pg. 54)
Eggless Challah (pg. 34)

Eggplant Caviar (pg. 43)
Whole Grain Crackers
Cherry Tomatoes or Grapes

Tabouli (pg. 86)
Pita Bread (pg. 36)
Lemonade (pg. 189)

DINNER SUGGESTIONS

Israeli Carrot Salad (pg. 75)
Bulgur "Meatballs" (pg. 91) or Chickpea Cutlets (pg. 93)
Pasta with Tomato Sauce
Steamed Broccoli
Apple Spice Cake (pg. 172)
Juice

Sliced Tomatoes and Cucumbers
Baked Falafel (pg. 90)
Baba Ghanoush (pg. 42)
Israeli Stuffed Grape Leaves (pg. 130)
Pita Bread (pg. 36)
Lemonade (pg. 189)

Radish and Tahini Salad (pg. 82)
Ruth's Eggless Kneidlach (pg. 67) and Vegetable Broth
    (pg. 70)
Polish Kasha and Mushrooms (pg. 107)
Baked Sweet Potato
Steamed Greens
Juice

Lentil Salad (pg. 78)
Indian Curry and Rice (pg. 101)
Stir-Fried Okra
Pita Bread (pg. 36) or Russian Flat Bread (pg. 41)
Mint Tea (pg. 190)

Garden Salad
Lebanese Green Bean and Chickpea Stew (pg. 103)
Baked White Potatoes
Almond Cookies (pg. 171)
Juice

Polish Dilled Cucumbers (pg. 81)
Romanian Mushroom Paprikash (pg. 110)
Steamed Zucchini
Pumpernickel Bread (pg. 38)
Fresh Fruit
Juice

Mixed Green Salad
Polish Plum and Rhubarb Soup (pg. 61) or Cream of
     Celery Soup (pg. 55)
Russian Mushroom Cutlets With Gravy (pg. 113)
Steamed Greens or Baked Carrots (pg. 138)
Sweet Fruit Kugel (pg.184)
Juice

Minted Split Pea Soup (pg. 58) or Armenian Tomato Soup
     (pg. 52)
Fruited Stuffed Peppers (pg. 128)
Potato Kugel (pg. 158)
Hamentashen (pg.177)
Juice

Turkish Mandarin Salad (pg. 87)
Vegetable Soup (pg. 71)
Seitan and Onions Over Mashed Potatoes (pg. 118)
Cake-Like Rye Bread (pg. 33) or Eggless Challah (pg. 34)
Juice

Russian Potato and Beet Salad (pg. 85)
Lentil Soup (pg. 57)
Stuffed Cabbage (pg. 133)
North African Pea Dish (pg. 154)
Apple Turnovers (pg. 173)
Lemonade (pg. 189)

Pineapple/Tangerine/Avocado Salad (pg. 80)
Hungarian Goulash (pg. 100) or Greek Okra Stew (pg. 98)
Steamed Corn or Yellow Squash
Italian Sautéed Chicory (pg. 149)
Greek Zucchini Pastries (pg. 176)
Juice

Tossed Salad
Sweet and Sour Cabbage Soup (pg. 68)
Herbed Lebanese Stew (pg. 99)
Steamed Greens
Syrian Wheat Pudding (pg. 185)
Lemonade (pg. 189)

ROSH HASHANAH DINNER IDEAS

Yemenite Bread Salad (pg. 88)
Potato Leek Soup (pg. 62)
Israeli Beans with Apples (pg. 102)
Romanian Sweet Pasta (pg. 160)
Italian Sautéed Chicory (pg. 149)
Romanian Apricot Dumplings (pg. 181)

Lebanese Green Bean Salad (pg. 76)
Romanian Tomato Soup (pg. 64)
Carrot Cutlets (pg. 92)
Vegetarian Cholent (pg. 123)
Steamed Broccoli
Rice Pudding (pg. 180)

Moroccan Beet Green Salad (pg. 79)
Turkish Potato Soup (pg. 69)
Russian Chickpea Bake (pg. 112)
Czechoslovakian Noodles with Poppy Seeds (pg. 95)
Steamed Squash
North African Barley Pudding (pg. 179)

PASSOVER SEDER IDEAS

Russian Charoset (pg. 83) With Matzo
Ruth's Eggless Kneidlach (pg. 67) and Vegetable Broth
    (pg. 70)
Eggplant Stew over Baked Potatoes (pg. 96)
Moroccan Beet Green Salad (pg. 79)
Syrian-Style Okra With Dried Fruit (pg. 168)
Russian Fruit Pudding (pg. 183)

Beet Salad (pg. 73)
Vegetable Soup (pg. 71)
Russian Potato and Mushroom Croquettes (pg. 116)
Broccoli and Lemon Dish (pg. 140)
Russian Cooked Cucumbers (pg. 162)
Fruit Compote (pg. 175)

Eggplant Spread (pg. 44) With Matzo
Russian Cold Borscht (pg. 65)
Passover Vegetarian Kishke (pg. 106)
Cabbage Sauté (pg. 142)
Russian Baked Peppers (pg. 161)
Sweet Potatoes
Baked Fruit

FIGURING FAT

Most health organizations recommend that you get no more than 30% of your *daily caloric intake* from fat. For many people, that advice is more confusing than helpful. For example, can you eat a dish that gets 60% of its calories from fat? What about foods like oil, that get all their calories from fat?

Yes, unless you have been put on a restricted diet, it is possible to eat the above items. The "30% or less of your daily calories from fat" guidelines does not refer to <u>individual</u> foods; it means <u>total</u> calories for the day. You can eat foods that get a high percentage of their calories from fat, and still eat a diet that is low in fat overall.

The best way to keep track of your fat intake is by counting grams of fat in a food, not the percentage of fat. During the course of a day, add up the total grams of fat you eat. Even if some foods you eat are high in fat, if the total number of grams for the day is low, you are doing okay.

If you had the choice between a food which had 50% of its calories from fat, but only one gram of fat; or a food with only 5% of its calories from fat, but 20 grams of fat, which food would cause you to consume more fat? The food with 20 grams of fat would be fattier.

Percentage of fat can also be confusing because they can be given either in relation to calories or in relation to the weight of a product. The resulting numbers are very different and consumers end up trying to compare apples to oranges.

Take 2% cow's milk as an example. It sounds like a lowfat

product, but that 2% figure is based on how many grams of fat there are in relation to the weight of a serving. If you figure out how many grams of fat there are in relation to calories, 2% milk is really 35% fat!

INTRODUCING FAT AS A PERCENTAGE OF DAILY VALUE

Fat as a percentage (%) of daily value is a figure being used on the new food labels. It compares the grams of fat in a food to a total maximum amount of grams of fat that you should be consuming during a day. (Note that this "maximum" amount is a compromise acceptable to the general population. You may want to aim lower.)

Fat as a percentage of daily value was conceived as a simple way to give the person who knows little or nothing about grams of fat an idea as to whether a food is high or low in fat. There are actually two values on the new food labels: One for a person who eats 2,000 calories and one for a person who consumes 2,500 calories per day. So, while keeping track of grams of fat is probably the best way to watch your fat intake, the fat as a percentage of daily value can be helpful in determining if a food is high or low in fat.

For this book, we have analyzed the recipes based on the 2,000 calorie figure/65 grams of fat per day. (You may want to eat less fat than that, particularly if you eat fewer calories.) Take our recipe for Barley Bean Soup as an example. It has 2 grams of fat. Based on a 2,000 calories/65 grams of fat per day, it fulfills 3% of the daily value for fat (2 divided by 65 = 3%).

TOP 10 DISHES FOR CALCIUM

Pumpernickel Bread (304 mg/svg) -- Page 38
Stuffed Cabbage (204 mg/svg) -- Page 133
Lebanese Potato Salad (174 mg/svg) -- Page 77
Parsley/Tahini Dip (150 mg/svg) -- Page 50
Spinach Knishes (134 mg/svg) -- Page 166
Israeli Beans with Apples (133 mg/svg) -- Page 102
Israeli Stuffed Grape Leaves (131 mg/svg) -- Page 130
Greek Okra Stew (125 mg/svg) -- Page 98
Noodles and Cabbage (122 mg/svg) -- Page 105
Yemenite Green Bean Stew (116 mg/svg) -- Page 124

How much calcium do we need? The Recommended Daily Allowance (RDA) for adults age 25 and older is 800 milligrams (mg) of calcium per day. An intake of 1,200 milligrams of calcium per day is recommended for those age 11 to 24. In other countries, calcium recommendations are lower than in the United States. For example, British adults are advised to have a calcium intake of 500 milligrams per day.

TOP 10 DISHES FOR IRON

Pumpernickel Bread (9.5 mg/svg) -- Page 38
Stuffed Cabbage (8.6 mg/svg) -- Page 133
Herbed Lebanese Stew (7.6 mg/svg) -- Page 99
Indian Curry and Rice (7 mg/svg) -- Page 101
Lentil Soup (6.1 mg/svg) -- Page 57
Greek Lentil Croquettes (5.6 mg/svg) -- Page 97
Turkish Black-Eyed Peas over Rice (5.5 mg/svg) --
    Page 121
Moroccan Chickpea and Lentil Soup (5.3 mg/svg) --
    Page 59
Eggplant Stew over Baked Potatoes (5.2 mg/svg) --
    Page 96
Fruit Compote (5 mg/svg) -- Page 175

How much iron do we need? The Recommended Daily Allowance (RDA) for adult men and for post-menopausal women is 10 milligrams of iron per day. Pre-menopausal women are advised to get 15 milligrams of iron per day.

BREADS & PANCAKES

BANANA BAGELS
(Makes 10)

Today, bagels can be found in supermarkets and bakeries throughout the United States. Often they contain sugar, eggs, and mostly white flour. In this recipe I use apple juice concentrate as a sweetener and a mashed banana for both a binder and additional sweetness. I also use mostly whole wheat pastry flour.

1-1/2 teaspoons active dry yeast
2 Tablespoons apple juice concentrate, at room
   temperature
3/4 cup warm water
1 cup unbleached white flour
2 ripe bananas, peeled and mashed
1/2 teaspoon salt
2-3/4 cups whole wheat pastry flour
8 cups or 2 quarts water

Mix together yeast, apple juice concentrate, and warm water in a large bowl. Add unbleached white flour. Mix ingredients well and allow to rise in a warm location for 15 minutes.

Add mashed banana, salt, and whole wheat pastry flour. Mix well and knead dough for 8 minutes, adding a little more flour if dough is too sticky.

Divide dough into 10 balls. Roll each ball between your palms to form approximately a 3/4-inch x 6-inch cylinder. Pinch ends of cylinder together to form a circle with a hole in the center (a bagel shape). Let bagels rise another 10 minutes.

Bring water to a boil in a large pot. Drop bagels 5 at a time into boiling water. Cook 1 minute, flip bagels over, and continue to boil for another 30 seconds. Remove bagels from water with slotted spoon and place onto a lightly oiled cookie sheet.

Preheat oven to 400 degrees. Bake bagels at 400 degrees for 30 minutes or until golden brown. Remove from oven and serve warm or cool.

Total calories per bagel: 180
Fat: 1 gram   Total Fat as % of Daily Value: 2%   Protein: 6 grams   Iron: 1.8 mg
Carbohydrates: 39 grams   Calcium: 18 mg   Dietary fiber: 5 grams

BLUEBERRY/BANANA MATZO MEAL PANCAKES
(Serves 4)

Matzo meal pancakes are traditionally served by American Jews during Passover. Usually they contain eggs and a sweetener may be added. I omit the eggs and substitute mashed bananas, which act both as a binder and sweetener. You can substitute other fruits such as chopped apples, peaches, pears, etc. for the blueberries.

4 ripe large bananas
1 cup blueberries
1 cup matzo meal
1 cup water
1-1/2 teaspoons oil

Mash bananas in a large bowl. Add remaining ingredients, except oil, and mix well.

Heat oil in a large non-stick skillet over medium heat. Pour half a ladle of batter at a time into pan to form 8 small pancakes. Cook pancakes 15 minutes on one side. Flip pancakes over and continue cooking for another 10 minutes. Serve warm.

Total calories per serving: 295
Fat: 3 grams Total Fat as % of Daily Value: 5% Protein: 5 grams Iron: 0.5 mg
Carbohydrates: 66 grams   Calcium: 11 mg   Dietary fiber: 4.6 grams

CAKE-LIKE RYE BREAD
(Serves 8)

Rye bread can be found in most Jewish bakeries. Instead of sugar, I use maple syrup and applesauce as the sweetener. Serve rye bread alone for breakfast or with a hearty stew or thick soup. It is quite filling, and this version can be prepared quicker than most rye breads.

1-1/2 cups rye flour
1/2 cup whole wheat pastry flour
1 cup unbleached white flour
1/4 cup maple syrup
1-1/2 teaspoons baking soda
1 teaspoon baking powder
1 teaspoon salt
2 Tablespoons caraway seeds
2 Tablespoons oil
1-1/4 cups applesauce
1/2 cup soy milk
1/2 cup water

Preheat oven to 350 degrees. Place all the ingredients in a large bowl. Mix well to form a dough. Place dough in a lightly oiled 9-1/4" x 5-1/4" x 3" loaf pan. Bake at 350 degrees for one hour. Remove bread from oven and allow it to cool slightly before removing from the pan. Serve bread warm.

Total calories per serving: 239
Fat: 5 grams   Total Fat as % of Daily Value: 7%   Protein: 6 grams   Iron: 1.8 mg
Carbohydrates: 44 grams   Calcium: 29 mg   Dietary fiber: 2.1 grams

EGGLESS CHALLAH

(Serves 12)

Traditionally, challah contains eggs, which presents a problem for individuals on restricted diets or those who choose not to eat eggs. This recipe instead uses Ener-G Egg Replacer, a powder consisting of a variety of starches, found in health food stores. You can also substitute corn or potato starch. Instead of sugar, I use apple juice concentrate as a sweetener. The challah will be a little heavier than traditional challah, which is often made out of white flour exclusively.

2-1/4 cups warm water
2 packages active dry yeast
1 Tablespoon unbleached white flour
1/3 cup apple juice concentrate, thawed
1 Tablespoon plus 2 teaspoons Ener-G Egg Replacer
1/4 cup oil (canola, safflower, etc.)
5 cups unbleached white flour
3 cups whole wheat pastry flour

Mix water, yeast, and 1 Tablespoon unbleached white flour in a large bowl. Cover bowl with a towel and let sit for 10 minutes in a draft-free location. Add remaining ingredients and knead mixture for 10 minutes, adding more flour as needed to make a firm dough. Knead until dough does not stick to your hands or board.

Pour 2 teaspoons of oil into bowl. Place dough in bowl and turn to coat slightly with oil. Set bowl in a draft-free, warm spot (80-100 degrees -- an oven that has been warmed and turned off works well) until double in size. This takes 1-1/2 hours.

Punch dough down and divide into 12 equal pieces. Roll each piece of dough to form a 9-inch long rope. Pinch 3 ropes together and braid them. Pinch end of braid. Repeat braiding process three more times. Place on lightly oiled baking sheet.

Cover the four small loaves with a towel and let them rise for 35 minutes. Preheat oven to 350 degrees. Then, bake challah for 35 minutes at 350 degrees. For an optional glazed topping, brush the loaves with a small amount of melted soy margarine before baking. Bread is best when served warm. Store leftovers in a plastic bag.

Total calories per serving: 335
Fat: 6 grams   Total Fat as % of Daily Value: 9%   Protein: 9 grams   Iron:3.3 mg
Carbohydrates: 62 grams   Calcium: 39 mg   Dietary fiber: 65 grams

PITA BREAD
(Serves 8)

Pita bread can be found in most supermarkets today, but is exceptionally delicious freshly homemade. It has been traditionally eaten by Jews in the Middle East. Once the dough has risen, it takes only a few minutes to bake. Pita bread can be served with various dips and spreads, stuffed with salads or burgers, or eaten alone.

1 Tablespoon active dry yeast
1-1/2 cups warm water
3 cups unbleached white flour
1-1/2 cups whole wheat pastry flour
1-1/2 teaspoons salt

Dissolve yeast in water and add to dry ingredients in a large bowl. Mix well and knead for 5 minutes. Cover bowl with a damp towel and let dough rise in a warm place for 3 hours.

Preheat oven to 375 degrees. Divide dough into 8 balls. Roll each ball out into a 6" wide x 1/2" thick circle. Place flattened dough onto an ungreased baking sheet. Bake at 375 degrees for 10 minutes until pita bread is light brown. Serve warm and store leftovers in a plastic bag.

Total calories per serving: 235
Fat: 1 gram   Total Fat as % of Daily Value: 1%   Protein: 8 grams   Iron: 2.8 mg
Carbohydrates: 49 grams   Calcium: 17 mg   Dietary fiber: 4 grams

POLISH APPLE BLINTZES
(Serves 3)

Blintzes are thin pancakes traditionally made with eggs and flour and stuffed with cheese, potatoes, or fruit. I eliminated the eggs and substituted cornstarch and a banana. Try other fruit or jams for the filling.

2 apples, cored and chopped finely
2 Tablespoons water
1/2 teaspoon cinnamon
3/4 cup unbleached white flour
1 cup soy milk
4 Tablespoons cornstarch
1 small banana, mashed

Place chopped apples, water, and cinnamon in a small pot. Simmer over a low heat for 15 minutes until apples become tender. Set mixture aside and allow to cool.

Meanwhile, blend the flour, soy milk, cornstarch, and banana in a blender or with a fork in a large bowl. Pour about 7 Tablespoons of batter into a small lightly oiled preheated frying pan. Spread batter around by tilting the pan. Cook over a medium heat until top is no longer moist. Scoop pancake out with a spatula and place it on a napkin to cool slightly. Repeat process until six pancakes have been made.

Do not to use too much oil or the blintzes will be greasy. If the pancake breaks, you are not cooking it long enough. If too crisp, you are overcooking the pancake.

Preheat oven to 350 degrees. Place 1/6 of apple mixture on each pancake and roll up the pancake. Place blintzes in a lightly oiled baking pan. Bake at 350 degrees for half hour until light brown. Serve two blintzes per person.

Total calories per serving: 275
Fat: 3 grams Total Fat as % of Daily Value: 5% Protein: 7 grams Iron: 2 mg
Carbohydrates: 57 grams Calcium: 41 mg Dietary fiber: 3.6 grams

PUMPERNICKEL BREAD
(Serves 8)

Pumpernickel bread is traditionally sourdough based and made primarily from rye flour. To get the dark color, bakers traditionally add coffee or carob powder. They also add a sweetener. I use black strap molasses, which gives the bread its dark color and serves as a sweetener along with mashed banana. I also use a combination of rye flour, whole wheat pastry flour, and cornmeal. This is a thick, dense bread that can be served alone, with soup, or with a vegetable stew.

2 packages active dry yeast (or 1 Tablespoon plus 1-1/2 teaspoons)
1-1/4 cup warm water
1 cup blackstrap molasses
2 ripe bananas, peeled and mashed
1 cup whole wheat pastry flour
1-1/2 cups cornmeal
5 cups rye flour
1 Tablespoon caraway seeds
1 teaspoon salt

Dissolve yeast in warm water and pour into a large bowl. Add molasses and mashed banana. Mix well. Slowly add remaining ingredients, mixing well as you go along to form a stiff dough. Add extra whole wheat pastry flour if the dough is too sticky. Knead dough for 5 minutes, then allow dough to rise in a warm, draft-free place for 1 hour. (The best method is to turn on your oven for a few minutes, turn it off, then let the dough rise in the warm oven.)

Punch dough down and place it in a lightly oiled one-pound loaf pan. Allow it to rise for another 15 minutes in a warm spot.

Preheat oven to 375 degrees. Bake bread for 1 hour at 375 degrees. Remove bread from oven and serve warm.

Total calories per serving: 487
Fat: 2 grams Total Fat as % of Daily Value: 3% Protein: 11 grams Iron: 9.5 mg
Carbohydrates: 109 grams   Calcium: 304 mg   Dietary fiber: 12.8 grams

RICE FLOUR PANCAKES
(Serves 4)

Traditional Greek rice flour pancakes contain eggs. Instead, I use mashed banana as a binder. The banana also acts as a sweetener. Brown rice flour can be purchased in natural foods markets.

2 cups brown rice flour
1 teaspoon baking soda
1/8 teaspoon salt
1 ripe banana, peeled and mashed
1/3 cup soy milk
1 cup water
2 teaspoons oil

Mix flour, baking soda, and salt together in a large bowl. Add mashed banana, soy milk, and water. Mix well.

Heat oil on a large griddle over medium heat. Pour 8 small pancakes onto heated pan. Cook 5 minutes. Carefully flip pancakes, and continue cooking for another 5 minutes. Serve warm.

Total calories per serving: 345
Fat: 5 grams Total Fat as % of Daily Value: 8% Protein: 7 grams Iron: 1.8 mg
Carbohydrates: 68 grams   Calcium: 17 mg   Dietary fiber: 4.2 grams

RUSSIAN FLAT BREAD

(Serves 8)

I've substituted molasses for the sugar and whole wheat pastry flour for white flour in this bread. Once the dough has risen, this is a very quick bread to prepare. Serve with spreads and/or with soup.

1 teaspoon active dry yeast
2 teaspoons molasses
1 Tablespoon oil
1-1/2 teaspoons salt
1-1/2 cups warm water
1-1/4 pounds whole wheat pastry flour

Mix yeast, molasses, oil, salt, and water together in a large bowl. Gradually add flour until dough is stiff. Knead dough 5 minutes and then place it in a lightly oiled bowl. Let dough rise in a warm location, covered with a damp cloth, for 1 hour.

Preheat oven to broil. Divide dough into 4 balls. Roll out each ball on a floured board to about a foot in diameter. Pierce flattened dough with a fork several times. Place on a cookie sheet and broil about 2 minutes on one side until brown. Turn bread over and broil 1 minute longer. Remove bread from oven and serve warm.

Total calories per serving: 257
Fat: 3 grams Total Fat as % of Daily Value: 5% Protein: 10 grams Iron: 2.5 mg
Carbohydrates: 52 grams   Calcium: 34 mg   Dietary fiber: 9 grams

DIPS & SPREADS

BABA GANOUJ
(Serves 8)

This popular Middle Eastern spread is often high in fat because of the large amount of tahini (sesame butter) added. I have cut back on the quantity of tahini used and instead added more lemon juice. The flavor remains delicious.

1 eggplant (about 1-1/2 pounds)
3 Tablespoons lemon juice
2 Tablespoons tahini (sesame butter)
2 cloves garlic, peeled and minced
1/4 cup fresh parsley, finely chopped
Salt and pepper to taste

Preheat oven to 375 degrees. Place several fork holes in eggplant. Place eggplant in baking dish and bake at 375 degrees for 1 hour until soft. Remove from oven, cut eggplant in half lengthwise and allow to cool. Once cool, remove skin and any large seeds from eggplant. Place cooked eggplant in a food processor bowl or blender cup. Add remaining ingredients and blend until smooth. Chill at least 1 hour before serving with pita bread.

Total calories per serving: 39
Fat: 1 gram   Total Fat as % of Daily Value: 2%   Protein: 2 grams   Iron: 1 mg
Carbohydrate: 7 grams   Calcium: 42 mg   Dietary fiber: 1 gram

EGGPLANT CAVIAR
(Serves 6)

This vegetarian caviar will please all your party guests.

1 large eggplant (over 2 pounds)
1 large onion, peeled and chopped
1 clove garlic, peeled and minced
1 green pepper, finely chopped
1 Tablespoon olive oil
2 tomatoes, peeled and chopped
2 Tablespoons dry wine or vinegar
1/3 cup water
Salt and pepper to taste

Preheat oven to 350 degrees. Poke several fork holes on one side of the eggplant. Place eggplant in a pan and bake at 350 degrees for 1 hour.

While the eggplant is baking, sauté onion, garlic and green pepper in oil for 4 minutes. Set aside.

Remove baked eggplant from oven, slit open with a knife, and allow it to cool. Once cool, peel the skin off the eggplant. Chop eggplant with tomatoes in a bowl. Add sautéed onion, garlic, and green pepper and mix well. Add wine or vinegar, water, and seasonings. Mix thoroughly and cool in refrigerator for at least one hour. Serve on whole wheat crackers.

Total calories per serving: 79
Fat: 3 grams   Total Fat as % of Daily Value: 5%   Protein: 3 grams   Iron: 1.5 mg
Carbohydrate: 13 grams   Calcium: 20 mg   Dietary fiber: 2.4 grams

EGGPLANT SPREAD
(Serves 6)

This lowfat eggplant spread takes on a distinctly different taste depending on whether you add fresh dill or parsley. You can serve this spread on matzo during Passover.

2 medium eggplants (about 2 pounds)
1 Tablespoon lemon juice
2 cloves garlic, peeled and minced
1 Tablespoon fresh dill or parsley, finely chopped
Salt and pepper to taste

Preheat oven to 375 degrees. Place eggplants in a baking pan. Poke several fork holes in each eggplant. Bake in 375 degree oven for 1 hour until soft. Remove from oven and allow to cool. Cut eggplants in half. Remove skin and any large seeds. Place cooked eggplant in a food processor bowl. Add remaining ingredients and blend until creamy. Chill before serving with pita bread or raw vegetables.

Total calories per serving: 41
Fat: <1 gram   Total Fat as % of Daily Value: <1%   Protein: 2 grams   Iron: 1.3 mg
Carbohydrate: 10 grams   Calcium: 29 mg   Dietary fiber: 1.4 grams

GREEK
FAVA BEAN SPREAD
(Serves 4)

Greek Jews often use fava beans in prepared dishes.

2 cups cooked fava beans, drained (19 ounce can)
2 scallions, finely chopped
1 teaspoon fresh dill, finely chopped
1 Tablespoon water
Salt and pepper to taste

Place all the ingredients in a food processor bowl. Blend until creamy. Chill and serve with pita bread, lettuce, and sliced tomato or with raw vegetables.

Total calories per serving: 94
Fat: <1 gram   Total Fat as % of Daily Value: <1%   Protein: 7 grams   Iron: 1.5 mg
Carbohydrate: 17 grams   Calcium: 40 mg   Dietary fiber: 0.9 grams

HUMMUS
(Serves 8)

Jews throughout the Middle East enjoy this chickpea spread.

4 cups pre-cooked chickpeas, drained (two 19-ounce cans)
1/2 cup water
3 Tablespoons tahini (sesame butter)
2 Tablespoons lemon juice
1 teaspoon sesame oil
1 teaspoon garlic powder
1 teaspoon cumin
Salt and pepper to taste

Place all the ingredients in a food processor bowl. Blend until creamy. Chill before serving with pita bread.

Total calories per serving: 171
Fat: 4 grams   Total Fat as % of Daily Value: 6%   Protein: 7 grams   Iron: 2 mg
Carbohydrate: 29 grams   Calcium: 80 mg   Dietary fiber: 4.5 grams

LEBANESE WALNUT SPREAD
(Serves 12)

This slightly spicy Lebanese spread is absolutely delicious. Serve in small portions.

2 cloves garlic, peeled and minced
1 cup walnuts
1 Tablespoon tahini
1/4 cup lemon juice
1 teaspoon salt
1/4 teaspoon cayenne pepper
2 Tablespoons water

Place garlic and walnuts in a food processor bowl and blend until finely chopped. Add remaining ingredients and blend until creamy. Serve small portions at room temperature or chilled on pita bread.

Total calories per serving: 70
Fat: 6 grams   Total Fat as % of Daily Value: 9%   Protein: 3 grams   Iron: 0.4 mg
Carbohydrate: 2 grams   Calcium: 17 mg   Dietary fiber: 0.6 grams

LENTIL PATÉ
(Serves 6)

This vegetarian paté is an excellent alternative to liver paté.

1 cup lentils
2-1/4 cups water
1 onion, peeled and finely chopped
4 cloves garlic, peeled and minced
2 teaspoons oil
1 teaspoon pepper
1/2 teaspoon vinegar
Water

Cook lentils in water over medium heat for 45 minutes. Meanwhile, sauté onion and garlic in oil for 2 minutes. When lentils are cooked, pour them into a food processor bowl. Add sautéed onion and garlic, pepper and vinegar. Blend in food processor until creamy, adding a little water if necessary. Chill and serve with pita bread, crackers, and/or raw vegetables.

Total calories per serving: 108
Fat: 2 grams   Total Fat as % of Daily Value: 3%   Protein: 7 grams   Iron: 2.6 mg
Carbohydrate: 17 grams   Calcium: 22 mg   Dietary fiber: 3.2 grams

MOCK CHOPPED "LIVER"
(Serves 6)

This is an excellent vegetarian alternative to chopped liver.

1/2 pound green beans, chopped in bite-size pieces
3/4 pound mushrooms, chopped
1 small onion, peeled and finely chopped
1 teaspoon oil
1/4 cup walnuts
Salt and pepper to taste
1/4 cup water

Sauté green beans, mushrooms, and onion in oil over medium-high heat for 10 minutes. Pour mixture into a food processor bowl. Add remaining ingredients and blend until creamy. Chill and serve on a bed of lettuce with pita bread or raw vegetables.

Total calories per serving: 67
Fat: 4 grams   Total Fat as % of Daily Value: 6% Protein: 3 grams   Iron: 1.2 mg
Carbohydrate: 6 grams   Calcium: 26 mg   Dietary fiber: 2.8 grams

PARSLEY/TAHINI DIP
(Serves 10)

This dip is very popular in Middle Eastern countries. Since tahini is high in fat, small portions of this dip should be spread on pita bread.

1-1/2 cups pre-cooked chickpeas, drained (15-ounce can)
3/4 cup tahini (sesame butter)
1-1/4 cups water
2 Tablespoons lemon juice
1 cup fresh parsley, finely chopped
1 teaspoon garlic powder
Salt to taste

Place all the ingredients in a food processor bowl and blend until creamy. Chill and serve small portions spread on pita bread.

Total calories per serving: 115
Fat: 6 grams   Total Fat as % of Daily Value: 9%   Protein: 4 grams   Iron: 2 mg
Carbohydrate: 14 grams   Calcium: 150 mg   Dietary fiber: 2.2 grams

ROMANIAN WHITE BEAN DIP
(Serves 8)

Jews from Romania often cook with white beans. Here white beans are used to prepare a delicious dip.

4 cups pre-cooked white beans, drained (two 19-ounce cans)
2 cloves garlic, minced
1/4 cup lemon juice
2 teaspoons olive oil
Salt and pepper to taste
1 teaspoon fresh parsley, finely chopped

Place all the ingredients (except parsley) in a food processor bowl. Blend until creamy. Garnish with finely chopped parsley. Chill before serving on bread or with raw vegetables.

Total calories per serving: 117
Fat: 2 grams   Total Fat as % of Daily Value: 3%   Protein: 7 grams   Iron: 1.9 mg
Carbohydrate: 19 grams   Calcium: 62 mg   Dietary fiber: 3 grams

SOUPS

ARMENIAN TOMATO SOUP
(Serves 8)

Adding bulgur to this tomato soup gives it a hearty flavor and a full-bodied texture.

4 ripe tomatoes, chopped
12 cups vegetable broth (see recipe on page 70)
1 cup bulgur (cracked wheat)
1/4 cup lemon juice
1 Tablespoon fresh mint, finely chopped (or 1 teaspoon dried)
10-ounce box frozen chopped spinach, thawed
Salt and pepper to taste

Place tomatoes, broth, and bulgur in a large pot and bring to a boil. Reduce heat, cover pot, and cook for 30 minutes. Add remaining ingredients and continue cooking for 15 minutes. Serve hot.

Total calories per serving: 122
Fat:2 grams   Total Fat as % of Daily Value:3%   Protein:6 grams   Iron:1.4 mg
Carbohydrates: 23 grams   Calcium:72 mg   Dietary fiber: 3.9 grams

BARLEY BEAN SOUP
(Serves 8)

You can substitute brown rice for the barley in this recipe.

1-1/4 cups barley
12 cups vegetable broth (see recipe on page 70)
1 onion, peeled and finely chopped
10-ounce box frozen lima beans
1 cup fresh parsley, finely chopped
Salt and pepper to taste

Cook barley in broth in a large covered pot over medium heat for 45 minutes. Add remaining ingredients and simmer 30 minutes longer. Serve hot.

Total calories per serving: 187
Fat:2 grams   Total Fat as % of Daily Value:3%   Protein:8 grams   Iron:2.1 mg
Carbohydrates: 35 grams   Calcium: 38 mg   Dietary fiber: 3.8 grams

COLD CHERRY SOUP
(Serves 4)

Traditionally sour cherries with a lot of added sugar are used in this recipe. I've substituted black sweet cherries and reduced the amount of added sweetener.

1 pound black sweet cherries
6 cups water
1/2 teaspoon powdered cloves
1/2 teaspoon cinnamon
2 Tablespoons cornstarch or potato starch for Passover
2 Tablespoons lemon juice
4 Tablespoons maple syrup

Remove pits from cherries and chop cherries in half. Place cherries in large pot with water, cloves, and cinnamon. Bring to a boil. Reduce heat and simmer 20 minutes. Dissolve cornstarch in lemon juice and add to pot. Add maple syrup and simmer for another 5 minutes, stirring occasionally. Refrigerate soup before serving.

Total calories per serving: 147
Fat: 1 gram   Total Fat as % of Daily Value: 2%   Protein: 1 gram   Iron: 0.5 mg
Carbohydrates: 35 grams   Calcium: 21 mg   Dietary fiber: 1.2 grams

CREAM OF CELERY SOUP

(Serves 6)

This delicious soup combines celery with a soy milk/vegetable broth base and a touch of dill weed.

1 carrot, peeled and finely chopped
1 potato, peeled and finely chopped
6 stalks celery, finely chopped
Small onion, peeled and finely chopped
2 teaspoons oil
2 cups lite (lowfat) soy milk
6 cups vegetable broth (see recipe on page 70)
1/2 teaspoon dill weed powder
Salt and pepper to taste

Sauté carrot, potato, celery, and onion with oil in a large pot over medium-high heat for 3 minutes. Take half of the sautéed vegetable mixture and place it in a blender cup. Add the soy milk and blend the mixture for 2 minutes. Return liquid to pot. Add vegetable broth, dill weed, and seasonings. Simmer over medium heat for 10 more minutes. Serve warm.

Total calories per serving: 99
Fat: 3 grams Total Fat as % of Daily Value: 5%   Protein: 4 grams   Iron: 0.4 mg
Carbohydrates: 16 grams   Calcium: 46 mg   Dietary fiber: 2.2 grams

CREAM OF MUSHROOM SOUP

(Serves 6)

This soup is traditionally made with cow's milk. Here I use soy milk and water.

3/4 pound mushrooms, chopped
2 stalks celery, chopped
1 large onion, peeled and finely chopped
2 teaspoons oil
2 cups soy milk
2 cups water
2 Tablespoons tamari or soy sauce
1/4 cup cornstarch
2 Tablespoons whole wheat flour
1/4 cup parsley, finely chopped
1/2 teaspoon celery seed
Dash of pepper

Sauté mushrooms, celery, and onion in oil in large pot over medium-high heat for 8 minutes. Add remaining ingredients and cook over medium heat, stirring often, until soup begins to thicken. Serve warm.

Total calories per serving: 120
Fat:4 grams   Total Fat as % of Daily Value:6%   Protein:6 grams   Iron:1.7 mg
Carbohydrates: 16 grams   Calcium: 46 mg   Dietary fiber: 2.3 grams

LENTIL SOUP
(Serves 8)

Adding chopped spinach to this soup is a wonderful addition to traditional lentil soup.

2 onions, peeled and chopped
2 cloves garlic, peeled and minced
2 teaspoons oil
1/2 teaspoon basil
1/2 teaspoon oregano
1 teaspoon fresh parsley, finely chopped
6 ounce can tomato paste
2 cups lentils
10 cups water
Salt to taste
1 pound fresh spinach, rinsed and chopped (or 10-
**   ounce package frozen spinach)**

Sauté onions and garlic in oil in large pot over medium-high heat for 2 minutes. Add remaining ingredients except spinach, cover, and simmer 40 minutes over medium heat. Add spinach. Cook 25 minutes longer until lentils are soft. Serve warm.

Total calories per serving: 182
Fat:2 grams   Total Fat as % of Daily Value:3%   Protein:13 grams   Iron:6.1 mg
Carbohydrates: 31 grams   Calcium: 94 mg   Dietary fiber: 7.9 grams

MINTED SPLIT PEA SOUP
(Serves 8)

Mint, commonly used in the Middle East, adds a special flavor to this thick soup.

10 cups water
2 cups green split peas
1 Tablespoon dried mint, crumbled
2 carrots, peeled and sliced thinly
1 onion, peeled and finely chopped
1/2 cup white basmati rice
1/2 teaspoon salt

Boil water in a large pot. Add split peas and dried mint, cover pot, and continue cooking over medium-high heat for 1 hour. Add remaining ingredients and cook 20 minutes longer. Serve hot.

Total calories per serving: 183
Fat: <1 gram   Total Fat as % of Daily Value: <1%   Protein: 10 grams   Iron: 2.4 mg
Carbohydrates: 36 grams   Calcium: 23 mg   Dietary fiber: 3.9 grams

MOROCCAN CHICKPEA AND LENTIL SOUP
(Serves 8)

This hearty soup can be served alone as a meal. You can substitute different cooked beans for the chickpeas.

1 large onion, peeled and finely chopped
3 stalks celery, finely chopped
2 teaspoons oil
2 cups lentils
14 cups water
2 cups pre-cooked chickpeas, drained (or a19-ounce can)
1 cup fresh cilantro, finely chopped
1 teaspoon cinnamon
1/2 teaspoon ginger
1/2 teaspoon turmeric
Salt and pepper to taste
3 ripe tomatoes, finely chopped
3 Tablespoons lemon juice

Sauté onion and celery with oil in a large pot over medium-high heat for 3 minutes. Add lentils and water. Cover pot and cook over medium heat for 40 minutes. Add chickpeas, cilantro, and seasonings. Cook 10 minutes longer. Finally, add tomatoes and lemon juice and cook for 10 more minutes. Serve hot.

Total calories per serving: 231
Fat:2 grams   Total Fat as % of Daily Value:3%   Protein:14 grams   Iron:5.3 mg
Carbohydrates: 41 grams   Calcium: 63 mg   Dietary fiber: 8 grams

POLISH MUSHROOM BARLEY SOUP
(Serves 10)

This soup is a meal in itself. Simply serve with a salad and fresh bread. Freeze leftovers.

2 cups barley
1 gallon plus 2 cups vegetable broth (see recipe on
    page 70)
2 potatoes, peeled and cubed
10-ounce box frozen baby lima beans
2 teaspoons oil
Small onion, peeled and finely chopped
3/4 pound mushrooms, chopped
3 stalks celery, finely chopped
1 teaspoon fresh dill, finely chopped
1/2 teaspoon paprika
Salt and pepper to taste

Cook barley in broth in a large covered pot over medium heat for 40 minutes. Add potatoes and lima beans. Continue cooking for another 20 minutes.

Meanwhile, sauté onion, mushrooms, and celery in oil in a large frying pan over medium heat for 5 minutes. Add sautéed vegetables to soup pot along with remaining ingredients. Cook 15 minutes longer and serve hot.

Total calories per serving: 259
Fat:3 grams   Total Fat as % of Daily Value:5%   Protein:10 grams   Iron:2.2 mg
Carbohydrates: 49 grams   Calcium: 36 mg   Dietary fiber: 5.6 grams

POLISH PLUM AND RHUBARB SOUP
(Serves 6)

Sugar is traditionally used in this heavenly scented soup. Instead I use apple juice concentrate. If the plums are not very sweet, you may want to add a bit more apple juice concentrate.

1 pound plums, pitted and chopped
1 pound rhubarb, chopped
10 cups water
1/4 cup plus 1 Tablespoon apple juice concentrate
1/4 teaspoon powdered cloves
1-1/2 teaspoons cinnamon

Place all the ingredients in a large pot and bring to a boil. Lower heat, cover pot, and simmer for 30 minutes. Serve hot.

Total calories per serving: 82
Fat: 1 gram   Total Fat as % of Daily Value: 2%   Protein: 1 gram   Iron: 0.4 mg
Carbohydrates: 20 grams   Calcium: 71 mg   Dietary fiber: 2.6 grams

POTATO LEEK SOUP
(Serves 10)

Traditionally this soup is made with cow's milk. I use soy milk instead.

5 potatoes, peeled and chopped
1 leek, including 3 inches of green tops, rinsed well and
    chopped
3 stalks celery, chopped
1/4 cup fresh dill weed, minced
8 cups or 2 quarts water
2 Tablespoons cornstarch
4 cups soy milk
1 teaspoon salt

Cook potatoes, leek, celery, and dill weed in water in a large covered pot over medium-high heat for 30 minutes. Dissolve cornstarch in soy milk. Pour into pot and add salt. Continue cooking over low heat for 10 minutes, stirring occasionally. Serve hot.

Total calories per serving: 143
Fat:3 grams   Total Fat as % of Daily Value:5%   Protein:6 grams   Iron:1 mg
Carbohydrates: 25 grams   Calcium: 43 mg   Dietary fiber: 2.2 grams

ROMANIAN KOHLRABI SOUP
(Serves 8)

A Romanian friend taught me how to prepare this recipe. Although it involves a bit of work to prepare, this soup is well worth the effort.

2 kohlrabi, peeled and diced
Small head of cauliflower, chopped
2 carrots, peeled and chopped
Small onion, peeled and finely chopped
1/2 cup fresh dill, finely chopped
1/2 cup fresh parsley, finely chopped
2 teaspoons oil
1/2 teaspoon thyme or basil
Salt and pepper to taste
1 Tablespoon cornstarch or potato starch for Passover
11 cups water
1/2 cup lemon juice or sauerkraut juice
15-ounce can tomato sauce

Stir-fry kohlrabi, cauliflower, carrots, onion, dill, and parsley in oil over medium-high heat in a large pot for 5 minutes. Add seasonings. Dissolve cornstarch in 1 cup water then add to the pot along with remaining 10 cups water. Bring to a boil then simmer covered for 30 minutes longer. Add lemon juice and tomato sauce and simmer another 15 minutes. Serve soup hot or chilled.

Total calories per serving: 66
Fat:2 grams   Total Fat as % of Daily Value:3%   Protein:3 grams   Iron:1.4 mg
Carbohydrates: 13 grams   Calcium: 45 mg   Dietary fiber: 4 grams

ROMANIAN TOMATO SOUP
(Serves 8)

This is a relatively simple, delicious soup to prepare. Serve with a dark bread.

1 cup brown rice
8 cups or 2 quarts vegetable broth (see recipe on page 70)
15-ounce can tomato sauce
4 ripe tomatoes, finely chopped
1/2 teaspoon paprika
Salt and pepper to taste

Place all the ingredients in a large covered pot. Simmer over medium-high heat for 55 minutes. Serve warm.

Total calories per serving: 135
Fat: 1 gram   Total Fat as % of Daily Value: 2%   Protein: 4 grams   Iron: 1.1 mg
Carbohydrates: 27 grams   Calcium: 26 mg   Dietary fiber: 3.7 grams

RUSSIAN COLD BORSCHT
(Serves 6)

This is a great cold soup to serve on a hot summer day when fresh beets and dill are widely available.

1 onion, peeled and finely chopped
6 beets, peeled and shredded (best done in a food processor)
2 Tablespoons wine vinegar
5 cups water
3 cups tomato juice
1/4 cup lemon juice
2 Tablespoons fresh dill, finely chopped
1/2 teaspoon garlic powder
Salt to taste

Mix all the ingredients together in a large pot. Bring mixture to a boil. Reduce heat, cover pot, and simmer 30 minutes. Chill in refrigerator before serving.

Total calories per serving: 45
Fat: <1 gram   Total Fat as % of Daily Value: <1%   Protein: 2 grams   Iron: 1.1 mg
Carbohydrates: 11 grams   Calcium: 22 mg   Dietary fiber: 2.5 grams

RUSSIAN SAUERKRAUT SOUP

(Serves 8)

The broth for this soup is a combination of tomato puree, vegetable broth, and sauerkraut juice. Add caraway seeds for flavor, and the end result is absolutely delicious. Root vegetables are eaten often in Russia.

15-ounce can tomato puree
8 cups or 2 quarts vegetable broth
16-ounce can or jar of sauerkraut
1 onion, peeled and finely chopped
2 turnips, peeled and cubed (about 1 pound)
3 carrots, peeled and finely chopped
1 teaspoon caraway seeds
Salt and pepper to taste

Place all the ingredients in a large covered pot and bring to a boil. Reduce heat and cook for 1 hour. Serve hot with fresh bread.

Total calories per serving: 73
Fat: 1 gram   Total Fat as % of Daily Value: 2%   Protein: 3 grams   Iron: 1.6 mg
Carbohydrates: 14 grams   Calcium: 65 mg   Dietary fiber: 4.7 grams

RUTH'S EGGLESS KNEIDLACH

(Serves 8)

Kneidlach are matzo balls. Traditionally they are made with eggs. This eggless version contains potatoes instead. Serve in vegetable broth (See page 70.)

4 medium potatoes, peeled and chopped
4 cups or 1 quart water
1-1/4 cups matzo meal
Pepper to taste

Boil potatoes in water in a large pot for 20 minutes until tender. Drain potatoes and mash them in a bowl. Add matzo meal and pepper. Knead dough until firm and smooth.

Fill a large pot 3/4 full with water. Bring to a boil. Form smooth 2-1/2" balls out of potato/matzo meal mixture. Drop balls into boiling water. Cook for 20 minutes in covered pot. Do not overcook! Carefully remove from water and serve kneidlech in hot vegetable broth.

Total calories per serving(without broth): 153
Fat: <1 gram   Total Fat as % of Daily Value: <1%   Protein: 4 grams   Iron: 0.3 mg
Carbohydrates: 34 grams   Calcium: 4 mg   Dietary fiber: 2.6 grams

SWEET AND SOUR CABBAGE SOUP

(Serves 6)

A combination of caraway seeds, tomato sauce, orange juice, and vinegar makes a delicious soup stock in this recipe. You can substitute different varieties of cabbage, too.

1 medium head of green cabbage, shredded
8 cups or 2 quarts water
1 Tablespoon caraway seeds
15-ounce can tomato sauce
2 Tablespoons orange juice concentrate
2 Tablespoons vinegar

Cook cabbage in water with caraway seeds and tomato sauce in a large pot over medium heat for 20 minutes. Add orange juice concentrate and vinegar. Simmer 5 minutes longer. Serve hot.

Total calories per serving: 56
Fat: <1 gram   Total Fat as % of Daily Value: <1%   Protein: 2 grams   Iron: 1.1 mg
Carbohydrates: 13 grams   Calcium: 56 mg   Dietary fiber: 5.8 grams

TURKISH POTATO SOUP
(Serves 6)

Adding fennel seed to this otherwise simple potato soup, gives it a unique taste. I also add soy milk.

1 onion, peeled and finely chopped
2 teaspoons oil
3 cups soy milk
5 cups vegetable broth (see recipe on page 70)
1 pound potatoes, peeled and cubed
2 carrots, peeled and finely chopped
1/2 teaspoon fennel seeds, crushed
1 teaspoon powdered ginger
1/2 cup fresh parsley, finely chopped
Salt and pepper to taste

Stir-fry onion with oil in a large pot over medium-high heat for 2 minutes. Add remaining ingredients and cook over medium-low heat for 45 minutes. Serve hot.

Total calories per serving: 189
Fat:6 grams   Total Fat as % of Daily Value:9%   Protein:8 grams   Iron:1.5 mg
Carbohydrates: 28 grams   Calcium: 69 mg   Dietary fiber: 2.7 grams

VEGETABLE BROTH
(Serves 8)

The secret to a good vegetable broth is to allow the vegetables to simmer slowly for several hours. This is a basic clear broth recipe. You can add or substitute other vegetables and herbs. If you prefer a red broth, simply add 6 ounces of tomato paste. This recipe freezes well.

10 cups water
1/2 medium onion, peeled and finely chopped
4 carrots, peeled and chopped
4 stalks celery, chopped
1 cup fresh parsley, finely chopped
1/4 teaspoon marjoram
Salt and pepper to taste
6 ounces tomato paste (optional)

Place all the ingredients in a large pot and bring to a boil. Reduce heat, cover pot, and simmer for 3 hours. Strain mixture if you prefer a clear broth. If you leave vegetables in broth, you have a simple vegetable soup. Serve hot.

Total calories per serving: 23
Fat: <1 gram   Total Fat as % of Daily Value: <1%   Protein: 1 gram   Iron: 0.8 mg
Carbohydrates: 5 grams   Calcium: 28 mg   Dietary fiber: 1.9 gram

VEGETABLE SOUP

(Serves 6)

This is a basic vegetable soup recipe. You can modify this recipe, depending upon the type of vegetables that are in season. Omit the peas or corn during Passover.

3 carrots, peeled and finely chopped
3 stalks celery, finely chopped
1 small zucchini, finely chopped
1 onion, peeled and finely chopped
2 teaspoons oil
8 cups or 2 quarts water
14-1/2-ounce can whole peeled tomatoes, chopped
1 cup fresh or frozen peas or corn kernels
1/4 cup fresh parsley, finely chopped
Salt and pepper to taste

Sauté carrots, celery, zucchini, and onion in oil in a large pot over medium-high heat for 5 minutes. Add water and bring to a boil. Reduce heat, cover pot, and simmer for 25 minutes. Add remaining ingredients and simmer 20 minutes longer. Serve hot.

Total calories per serving: 78
Fat:2 grams   Total Fat as % of Daily Value:3%   Protein:3 grams   Iron:1.4 mg
Carbohydrates: 14 grams   Calcium: 53 mg   Dietary fiber: 5 grams

YEMENITE GREEN BEAN SOUP
(Serves 6)

This is a wonderful soup recipe to prepare when you don't know what to do with all the fresh green beans you've grown in your garden.

1 cup brown rice
2-1/2 cups water
1 pound green beans, chopped
1 small onion, peeled and finely chopped
2 teaspoons oil
6 cups tomato juice
2 cups water
Salt and pepper to taste

Cook brown rice in 2-1/2 cups water in a covered pot over medium-low heat for 35 minutes.

Meanwhile, sauté green beans and onion in oil in a large pot over medium-high heat for 5 minutes. Add juice, water, and seasonings. Bring to a boil. Reduce heat and simmer over medium heat for 20 minutes. Add cooked rice and simmer 5 minutes longer. Serve hot.

Total calories per serving: 194
Fat:2 grams   Total Fat as % of Daily Value:3%   Protein:6 grams   Iron:2.6 mg
Carbohydrates: 41 grams   Calcium: 71 mg   Dietary fiber: 5 grams

SALADS

BEET SALAD
(Serves 6)

A combination of horseradish and beets along with fresh dill makes this a unique salad.

**4 cups cooked fresh beets, grated or finely chopped
(two 16-ounce cans, drained)
2 teaspoons prepared horseradish
2 Tablespoons vinegar
2 Tablespoons orange juice concentrate
2 Tablespoons fresh dill, finely minced**

Mix all the ingredients together in a large bowl. Chill and toss once before serving.

Total calories per serving: 46
Fat: <1 gram   Total Fat as % of Daily Value: <1%   Protein: 1 gram   Iron: 0.7 mg
Carbohydrate: 10 grams   Calcium: 15 mg   Dietary fiber: 2.9 grams

BULGUR AND GRAPE SALAD
(Serves 6)

This is an absolutely delicious salad and well worth the wait while the bulgur soaks in the juice. The salad can even be served for breakfast! Experiment with different types of juices and other fruits such as chopped apples, peaches, or pears.

2 cups bulgur
4 cups orange juice
1 pound seedless grapes (To make a colorful salad, use different varieties of grapes.)
2 teaspoons cinnamon

Soak bulgur in juice for at least 4-1/2 hours until the juice is absorbed and the bulgur is soft. (You can soak the mixture overnight if you prefer.)

Cut grapes in half and toss into the soaked bulgur. Add cinnamon and stir well. Chill and toss once before serving.

Total calories per serving: 313
Fat: 1 gram   Total Fat as % of Daily Value: 2%   Protein: 8 grams   Iron: 1.9 mg
Carbohydrate: 70 grams   Calcium: 46 mg   Dietary fiber: 5.7 grams

ISRAELI CARROT SALAD
(Serves 8)

Oranges are a leading crop in Israel. Here they are added to grated carrots, along with mint and raisins, to create the very popular Israeli carrot salad.

2-1/2 pounds carrots, peeled and grated
5 Temple oranges, peeled, sectioned, and chopped
Juice of one lemon
2 Tablespoons dried mint
1 cup raisins

Toss all the ingredients together in a large bowl. Chill before serving.

Total calories per serving: 136
Fat: <1 gram   Total Fat as % of Daily Value: <1%   Protein: 3 grams   Iron: 1.3 mg
Carbohydrate: 34 grams   Calcium: 110 mg   Dietary fiber: 8.6 grams

LEBANESE GREEN BEAN SALAD
(Serves 5)

This is a great recipe to use in late spring or fall when you don't know what to do with all those fresh green beans left in your garden (or on your local supermarket shelf).

1 pound fresh green beans, ends removed
2 cloves garlic, peeled and minced
Small onion, peeled and finely chopped
2 Tablespoons lemon juice
2 teaspoons olive oil
2 Tablespoons fresh parsley, finely chopped
Salt and pepper to taste

Snap beans in half and steam over boiling water for 8 minutes until tender. Place steamed beans in a large bowl. Stir in remaining ingredients and mix well. Chill for at least 2 hours before serving.

Total calories per serving: 48
Fat: 2 grams   Total Fat as % of Daily Value: 3%   Protein: 2 grams   Iron: 0.9 mg
Carbohydrate: 8 grams   Calcium: 48 mg   Dietary fiber: 2.4 grams

LEBANESE POTATO SALAD

(Serves 12)

Instead of mayonnaise, a creamy tahini (sesame butter) dressing is used in this recipe to create a delicious potato salad. This can be served as a main dish.

4 pounds white potatoes, washed and chopped
10 cups water
1 cup fresh parsley, finely chopped
4 scallions, finely chopped
1 clove garlic, peeled and minced
1 cup tahini (sesame butter)
1/4 cup lemon juice
1 cup water
1 teaspoon salt

Cook potatoes in 10 cups water until tender. Drain and allow potatoes to cool.

Once the potatoes have cooled, toss them with the parsley and scallions in a large bowl. Place the garlic, tahini, lemon juice, 1 cup water, and salt in a blender cup (or large bowl if you do not use a blender). Blend or stir dressing ingredients until creamy. Pour tahini dressing over the potato mixture. Toss well and serve either at room temperature or chilled.

Total calories per serving: 265
Fat:6 grams   Total Fat as % of Daily Value:9%   Protein:6 grams   Iron:4 mg
Carbohydrate: 49 grams   Calcium: 174 mg   Dietary fiber: 4.6 grams

LENTIL SALAD
(Serves 6)

This hearty salad is quite popular in the Middle East, where lentils are found in abundance in most marketplaces.

1-1/2 cups lentils
3-1/2 cups water
1 onion, peeled and finely chopped
Salt and pepper to taste
1 teaspoon coriander
3 scallions, finely chopped
2 teaspoons olive oil
1 Tablespoon lemon juice

Cook the lentils in water with the chopped onion in a large pot over medium heat for 45 minutes until lentils are soft. Drain any excess water and allow lentils to cool. Mash half the lentils and stir back into remaining lentils. Add seasonings, and scallions. Drizzle oil and lemon juice over lentils. Stir well and chill before serving.

Total calories per serving: 152
Fat: 2 grams   Total Fat as % of Daily Value: 3%   Protein: 10 grams   Iron: 4 mg
Carbohydrate: 25 grams   Calcium: 32 mg   Dietary fiber: 5 grams

MOROCCAN BEET GREENS SALAD

(Serves 3)

*Few people know what to do with beet greens other than steam them.
Prepared that way they often seem bitter to Americans. Adding a little
garlic, paprika, and lemon juice makes this excellent salad.*

Greens from 3 beets including stems
1 teaspoon olive oil
1 Tablespoon water
1 clove garlic, peeled and minced
1/2 teaspoon paprika
1/4 teaspoon salt
1 Tablespoon lemon juice

Separate beet stems from leaves and chop both. Sauté the beet stems with oil and
water in a large frying pan over medium-high heat for 3 minutes. Add chopped beet
leaves and remaining ingredients (except lemon juice) and sauté 5 minutes longer.
Add lemon juice and sauté 1 more minute. Serve warm or chilled.

Total calories per serving: 34
Fat: 2 grams   Total Fat as % of Daily Value: 3%   Protein: 2 grams   Iron: 1.4 mg
Carbohydrate: 5 grams   Calcium: 84 mg   Dietary fiber: 2.1 grams

PINEAPPLE, AVOCADO, AND TANGERINE SALAD
(Serves 5)

This simple salad is absolutely delicious.

**2 cups fresh pineapple, chopped into bite-size pieces
(or 15-1/2 ounce can juice-packed pineapple
chunks, drained)
1 ripe avocado, peeled, pit removed, and diced
2 tangerines, peeled, seeds removed, and sections cut
into thirds**

Toss all the ingredients together in a large bowl. Chill before serving on a bed of lettuce.

Total calories per serving: 110
Fat: 6 grams   Total Fat as % of Daily Value: 9%   Protein: 1 gram   Iron: 0.7 mg
Carbohydrate: 14 grams   Calcium: 13 mg   Dietary fiber: 2 grams

POLISH DILLED CUCUMBERS
(Serves 8)

Now in her nineties, my grandmother still makes Polish dilled cucumbers. She uses more salt than I have used in this recipe, calls for sugar instead of corn or rice syrup, and prefers onions over chopped scallions. My mother uses chives instead of onions or scallions. In any case, this recipe is well worth the time it takes to prepare.

3 cucumbers, peeled and sliced in 1/4-inch thick rounds
1 teaspoon salt
2-1/2 cups water
1/2 cup vinegar
1/4 cup corn or rice syrup
3 scallions, finely chopped
1/8 teaspoon pepper

Place sliced cucumber rounds on a flat plate one layer at a time, sprinkling some salt on each layer. Put another flat plate on top. Place a heavy weight on top of the plate and allow cucumbers to sit for at least 3 hours.

Heat water with vinegar and corn or rice syrup until it boils. Turn off heat and allow liquid to cool.

Rinse cucumbers with cold water after they have sat at least 3 hours. Place rinsed cucumbers in a large jar. Add liquid mixture and scallions and pepper. Chill in closed jar overnight and serve cold.

Total calories per serving: 47
Fat: <1 gram   Total Fat as % of Daily Value: <1%   Protein: 1 gram   Iron: 0.8 mg
Carbohydrate: 11 grams   Calcium: 22 mg   Dietary fiber: 1.6 grams

RADISH TAHINI SALAD
(Serves 4)

Radishes are found in every supermarket and yet most people don't know how to use them creatively in a salad. Here radishes are grated and a tahini/lemon juice dressing is poured over them along with fresh parsley.

6 ounces radishes (about 12), leaves and roots removed
1 Tablespoon tahini (sesame butter)
2 Tablespoons lemon juice
1 teaspoon olive oil
1/4 cup fresh parsley, finely chopped
Salt and pepper to taste

Grate radishes in a food processor or by hand with a grater. Toss with the remaining ingredients in a large bowl. Chill at least one hour and serve on a bed of lettuce or bean sprouts.

Total calories per serving: 29
Fat: 2 grams   Total Fat as % of Daily Value: 3%   Protein: 1 gram   Iron: 0.5 mg
Carbohydrate: 2 grams   Calcium: 36 mg   Dietary fiber: 0.6 grams

RUSSIAN CHAROSET

(Serves 8)

This dish is traditionally served during Passover by Russian Jews. If fresh apricots are not available, you may substitute 1-1/2 cups dried apricots that have been chopped.

1 pound pears (2-3 pears), cored and grated
1 pound apricots (7-8 apricots), pitted and finely grated
2 Tablespoons slivered almonds

Toss all the ingredients together in a bowl. Chill and stir before serving.

Total calories per serving: 72
Fat: 1 gram   Total Fat as % of Daily Value: 2%   Protein: 1 gram   Iron: 0.5 mg
Carbohydrate: 15 grams   Calcium: 19 mg   Dietary fiber: 2.8 g rams

RUSSIAN EGGPLANT AND POMEGRANATE SALAD
(Serves 6)

Although this dish takes some time to prepare, it is unique and worth the effort. Pomegranate is popular in the Middle East, North Africa, the Mediterranean area, and parts of China.

1 or 2 eggplants (about 2 pounds), peeled and chopped
1/4 teaspoon basil
1/4 teaspoon coriander
1/4 teaspoon garlic powder
1/4 teaspoon paprika
1/4 teaspoon salt
1/4 cup fresh parsley, finely chopped
1/2 small onion, peeled and finely chopped
2 teaspoons olive oil
1/2 cup water
2 pomegranates, seeds removed and saved

Heat all the ingredients except pomegranate seeds together in a large covered pot over medium heat for 20 minutes, stirring occasionally. Add pomegranate seeds and chill before serving on a bed of lettuce.

Total calories per serving: 89
Fat: 2 grams   Total Fat as % of Daily Value: 3%   Protein: 2 grams   Iron: 1.4 mg
Carbohydrate: 18 grams   Calcium: 24 mg   Dietary fiber: 1.8 grams

RUSSIAN POTATO AND BEET SALAD
(Serves 6)

This unique Russian potato salad is quite colorful.

3 fresh beets, peeled and cubed
5 cups water
4 potatoes, peeled and cubed
4 cups water
2 carrots, peeled and finely chopped
Small onion, peeled and finely chopped
2 sour pickles, chopped
Salt to taste

Cook beets with 5 cups water in a pot over medium heat for 1 hour. In a separate pot cook potatoes with 4 cups water over medium heat for 20 minutes. Add carrots and onion to potatoes and continue cooking 20 minutes longer. Drain beets and drain cooked potato/carrot/onion mixture. Toss ingredients together in a large bowl. Add pickles and seasonings. Chill before serving.

Total calories per serving: 104
Fat: <1 gram   Total Fat as % of Daily Value: <1%   Protein: 2 grams   Iron: 0.9 mg
Carbohydrate: 24 grams   Calcium: 28 mg   Dietary fiber: 3.9 grams

TABOULI

(Serves 6)

This popular Middle Eastern salad is beautiful to the eye when presented, and quite filling. You can serve it on a bed of lettuce or in pita bread as a sandwich filling.

1 cup bulgur
2 cups water
1/2 cup fresh parsley, finely chopped
1/2 cup scallions, finely chopped (2-3 scallions)
2 Tablespoons fresh mint, finely chopped, or two
    teaspoons dried mint
1 Tablespoon olive oil
1/4 cup lemon juice
1 teaspoon cinnamon
Salt and pepper to taste
1 large tomato, chopped
1 cucumber, peeled and finely chopped

Soak bulgur with water in a large bowl for at least one hour. (The bulgur will greatly expand as it absorbs the liquid; so be certain to use a large bowl.) Add remaining ingredients and toss well. Chill before serving.

Total calories per serving: 131
Fat: 3 grams   Total Fat as % of Daily Value: 5%   Protein: 4 grams   Iron: 1.5 mg
Carbohydrate: 24 grams   Calcium: 33 mg   Dietary fiber: 4.1 grams

TURKISH
MANDARIN SALAD
(Serves 5)

This salad incorporates a wide variety of foods and spices.

Two 10-1/2 ounce cans Mandarin oranges, drained
1/2 Spanish onion, peeled and finely chopped
1/4 cup pitted black olives, chopped
1/4 cup pitted green olives, chopped
1/2 teaspoon coriander
1/2 teaspoon paprika
Salt and pepper to taste

Toss all the ingredients together in a large bowl. Chill and serve over a bed of lettuce.

Total calories per serving: 96
Fat: 2 grams   Total Fat as % of Daily Value: 3%   Protein: 1 gram   Iron: 0.6 mg
Carbohydrate: 22 grams   Calcium: 18 mg   Dietary fiber: 1.4 grams

YEMENITE BREAD SALAD
(Serves 10)

This is an absolutely delicious hearty salad.

6 small whole wheat pita breads (or 3 large)
1 pound (approx.) romaine lettuce, torn into bite-size
    pieces
2 scallions, finely chopped
1 cucumber, peeled and chopped into cubes
2 ripe tomatoes, chopped
1/2 cup fresh parsley, minced
1 Tablespoon dried mint
2 Tablespoons lemon juice
1/4 cup olive oil
1 chili pepper, finely chopped (optional)

Cut pita bread into bite-size pieces and toast in toaster oven or under broiler for a few minutes. Toss lettuce, scallions, cucumber, tomato, parsley, and mint in a large bowl. Add lemon juice and olive oil. Toss again. Add bread right before serving and toss one more time.

Total calories per serving: 128
Fat: 6 grams   Total Fat as % of Daily Value: 9%   Protein: 4 grams   Iron: 1.5 mg
Carbohydrate: 16 grams   Calcium: 47 mg   Dietary fiber: 2 grams

MAIN DISHES

ARMENIAN SPINACH AND BULGUR DISH
(Serves 6)

Bulgur is wheat that has been cooked, dried, and then coarsely ground. It expands a lot as it absorbs liquid while cooking.

1 large onion, peeled and finely chopped
2 teaspoons oil
2 cups bulgur
6 cups water
3 ripe tomatoes, chopped
1/2 pound fresh spinach, chopped
Salt and pepper to taste

Sauté onion in oil in large frying pan over medium-high heat for 3 minutes. Add bulgur and water. Simmer over medium heat for 10 minutes. Add tomatoes, spinach, and seasonings. Continue simmering for 15 minutes longer, stirring occasionally. Serve dish hot.

Total calories per serving: 228
Fat: 3 grams   Total Fat as % of Daily Value: 5%   Protein: 9 grams   Iron: 2.9 mg
Carbohydrate: 45 grams   Calcium: 69 mg   Dietary fiber: 7.8 grams

BAKED FALAFEL
(Serves 6)

Anyone who has visited Israel knows that falafel is a staple dish there. Serve it on a bed of lettuce with chopped tomato and cucumber, and tahini sauce. You can also serve it in pita bread. Children especially love falafel sandwiches.

4 cups pre-cooked chickpeas, drained (two 19-ounce cans)
1 teaspoon dill weed powder
1/2 cup fresh parsley, finely chopped
1 small onion, peeled and minced
1 teaspoon garlic powder
1 Tablespoon baking soda
1 teaspoon cumin
1/8 teaspoon cayenne pepper
2 Tablespoons sesame seeds

Preheat oven to 400 degrees. Mash chickpeas in a bowl and add the remaining ingredients. Mix well.

Divide mixture into 24 one-inch balls. Flatten each ball with your palm and place on a lightly oiled cookie sheet. Bake at 400 degrees for 35 minutes and turn the falafel over. Continue baking another 15 minutes. Serve 4 falafels per person.

Total calories per serving: 214
Fat: 3 grams   Total Fat as % of Daily Value: 5%   Protein: 9 grams   Iron: 3 mg
Carbohydrate: 38 grams   Calcium: 90 mg   Dietary fiber: 6.4 grams

BULGUR "MEATBALLS"
(Serves 4)

This dish is a unique healthy alternative to meatballs.

1 cup bulgur
3 cups water
1/2 cup whole wheat flour
1 carrot, peeled and grated
3 scallions, finely chopped
2 Tablespoons parsley, finely chopped
1 teaspoon tamari
1/2 teaspoon garlic powder
1 Tablespoon oil

Soak bulgur in water in large bowl for 2 hours. Using your hands, squeeze out any excess water left in the bulgur.

Mix soaked bulgur with the remaining ingredients, except the oil. Form mixture into 16 round balls.

Heat oil in frying pan over medium-high heat. Cook "meatballs" in oil, turning every few minutes, until brown on all sides. Remove from pan. Lay the "meatballs" on piece of paper towel to drain excess oil off. Serve 4 "meatballs" per person along with brown rice, pasta, or mashed potatoes.

Total calories per serving: 234
Fat: 4 grams   Total Fat as % of Daily Value: 6%   Protein: 8 grams   Iron: 2 mg
Carbohydrate: 43 grams   Calcium: 38 mg   Dietary fiber: 6.8 grams

CARROT CUTLETS

(Serves 6)

My mother created this delicious dish. The cutlets can be served plain or with an onion or mushroom sauce.

2 cups pre-cooked brown rice or millet
1 small onion, peeled and finely chopped
1 Tablespoon fresh parsley, finely chopped
1 cup carrots, cooked and mashed (about 3 raw
      carrots)
1 Tablespoon water or soy milk
2 Tablespoons cornstarch
3/4 cup wheat germ
2 Tablespoons oil

Mix all the ingredients together in a bowl, except for the oil. Form 12 small patties.

Heat oil in a large frying pan over medium heat. Fry carrot cutlets for 5 minutes or until brown on one side. Flip over and continue frying for another 5 minutes. Serve cutlets warm, 2 per serving.

Variation: Instead of frying the cutlets, you can bake them on a lightly oiled pan in a 425-degree oven until brown on one side. Flip the cutlets and continue baking 5 minutes longer.

Total calories per serving: 177
Fat: 6 grams   Total Fat as % of Daily Value: 9%   Protein: 4 grams   Iron: 1.4 mg
Carbohydrate: 28 grams   Calcium: 27 mg   Dietary fiber: 2.9 grams

CHICKPEA CUTLETS
(Serves 9)

This dish is an excellent alternative to veal cutlets. Serve with your favorite pasta and tomato sauce.

6 cups pre-cooked chickpeas, drained (three 19-ounce cans)
4 carrots, peeled and grated
1 onion, peeled and chopped finely
4 stalks celery, chopped finely
Salt and pepper to taste
3/4 cup whole wheat pastry flour
1 Tablespoon oil

Mash the chickpeas, then mix all the ingredients together, except the oil. Form eighteen 3-inch patties and fry in oil in pan over medium heat until brown on both sides. Serve warm with tomato sauce over pasta.

Total calories per serving: 258
Fat: 4 grams   Total Fat as % of Daily Value: 6%   Protein: 10 grams   Iron: 2.8 mg
Carbohydrate: 48 grams   Calcium: 73 mg   Dietary fiber: 8.5 grams

CHICKPEA TURNOVERS
(Serves 8)

These hearty turnovers are sure to warm you up on a cold day.

4 cups pre-cooked chickpeas, drained (or two 19-ounce cans)
2 teaspoons oil
1 onion, peeled and finely chopped
2 teaspoons curry powder
1 tomato, chopped
2 Tablespoons margarine
16 sheets of phyllo dough

Mash half the chickpeas in a bowl and set aside.

Heat oil in a large pan over medium-high heat and sauté onion with curry powder for 1 minute. Add chickpeas (whole and mashed) and chopped tomato. Sauté mixture for 2 minutes longer.

Preheat oven to 375 degrees. Meanwhile, melt margarine in a small pot and set aside. Remove 4 sheets of phyllo dough and cut into 4 equal rectangles. Place approximately 1/4 cup of the chickpea mixture in the center of each rectangle. Fold ends of phyllo dough in. Repeat process with remaining phyllo dough to make 16 turnovers.

Place turnovers on a lightly oiled cookie sheet. Brush with melted margarine and bake for 35 minutes at 375 degrees until brown on top. Serve 2 turnovers per person.

Total calories per serving: 301
Fat: 6 grams   Total Fat as % of Daily Value:9%   Protein:11 grams   Iron:3.3 mg
Carbohydrate: 55 grams   Calcium: 56 mg'   Dietary fiber: 4.7 grams

CZECHOSLOVAKIAN NOODLES WITH POPPY SEEDS
(Serves 6)

Traditionally this dish would be made with cream, and a sweetener would be added. Instead, I use vanilla soy milk and water to reduce the overall fat content of this delicious dish. If you are unable to purchase vanilla soy milk, simply add a few drops of vanilla to plain soy milk.

12-ounce package eggless noodles
10 cups water
1 Tablespoon poppy seeds
1-1/2 cups vanilla soy milk
1/2 cup water
2 Tablespoons cornstarch
1/4 teaspoon salt

Cook noodles in 10 cups boiling water for 8-10 minutes until done. Drain noodles.
    Meanwhile, put remaining ingredients in a separate pot and bring to a boil, stirring constantly. Reduce heat and simmer 2 minutes, stirring continuously. Remove from heat, add cooked noodles, and serve warm.

Total calories per serving: 211
Fat:3 grams   Total Fat as % of Daily Value:5%   Protein:8 grams   Iron:1.8 mg
Carbohydrate: 38 grams   Calcium: 54 mg   Dietary fiber: 1.2 grams

EGGPLANT STEW OVER BAKED POTATOES
(Serves 8)

This dish can be served during Passover or year-round.

8 large baking potatoes
2 large eggplants, peeled and cubed
1 large onion, peeled and finely chopped
2 Tablespoons oil
1/4 cup water
One 28-ounce can tomato sauce
1 teaspoon garlic powder
Salt and pepper to taste

Preheat oven to 400 degrees. Bake potatoes for 1 hour at 400 degrees until done.

Meanwhile, in a separate pan, sauté eggplant and onion in oil and water over medium heat until the eggplant is tender. Add tomato sauce and spices. Simmer 5 minutes longer and serve over baked potatoes.

Total calories per serving: 344
Fat: 4 grams   Total Fat as % of Daily Value: 6%   Protein: 9 grams   Iron: 5.2 mg
Carbohydrate: 73 grams   Calcium: 66 mg   Dietary fiber: 9.9 grams

GREEK LENTIL CROQUETTES

(Serves 4)

Fresh or dried mint adds wonderful flavor to these croquettes.

1 cup lentils
3 cups water
1 small onion, peeled and finely chopped
1 cup bulgur
1/2 cup fresh parsley, finely chopped
1/4 cup fresh mint, finely chopped or 3 Tablespoons
   dried mint
1 teaspoon cumin
1 Tablespoon lemon juice
1 Tablespoon oil

Cook lentils in water with onion over medium heat for 35 minutes. Add bulgur, parsley, mint, and cumin. Continue cooking 10 minutes longer, stirring occasionally to prevent sticking.

Remove mixture from the heat. Stir in lemon juice and allow mixture to cool.

Form 8 croquettes and fry in oil over medium-high heat for 5 minutes. Gently flip croquettes and fry 5 minutes longer. Serve 2 croquettes per person.

Total calories per serving: 312
Fat: 4 grams   Total Fat as % of Daily Value: 6%   Protein: 16 grams   Iron: 5.6 mg
Carbohydrate: 54 grams   Calcium: 58 mg   Dietary fiber: 8.9 grams

GREEK OKRA STEW
(Serves 4)

Traditionally beef is used in this okra dish. Here I've substituted seitan for meat to create a delicious vegetarian alternative.

1 onion, peeled and chopped
2 teaspoons oil
1 pound okra, chopped
8-ounce package seitan, drained and cubed
2 tomatoes, chopped
2 Tablespoons red wine vinegar
2 Tablespoons lemon juice
1/2 teaspoon garlic powder
1/2 teaspoon coriander
Salt and pepper to taste

Stir-fry onion with oil in a large frying pan over medium heat for 3 minutes. Add okra and remaining ingredients. Stir-fry 10 minutes longer. Serve hot over cooked brown rice.

Total calories per serving: 152
Fat: 3 grams   Total Fat as % of Daily Value: 5%   Protein: 14 grams   Iron: 3.1 mg
Carbohydrate: 20 grams   Calcium: 125 mg   Dietary fiber: 2.4 grams

HERBED LEBANESE STEW
(Serves 6)

This hearty stew includes red lentils, which cook quicker than the more common greenish brown lentils.

2-1/2 cups red lentils
5 cups water
1 Tablespoon oil
1 onion, peeled and finely chopped
3 Tablespoons fresh cilantro, finely chopped
3 white potatoes, peeled and cubed into small pieces
2 cups pre-cooked chickpeas, drained (19-ounce can)
1-1/2 cups water
3 Tablespoons lemon juice
1/4 teaspoon cayenne
Salt to taste

Cook lentils with 5 cups of water in a covered pot for 20 minutes over medium heat.

Meanwhile, sauté onion with oil in a large pot over medium heat for 3 minutes. Add cilantro and potatoes. Stir-fry for 5 minutes. Add chickpeas and water. Cover and simmer 15 minutes longer, stirring occasionally.

Add cooked lentils with liquid, lemon juice, cayenne, and salt. Simmer 5 more minutes, stirring occasionally. Serve warm.

Total calories per serving: 399
Fat: 4 grams   Total Fat as % of Daily Value: 6%   Protein: 22 grams   Iron: 7.6 mg
Carbohydrate: 71 grams   Calcium: 72 mg   Dietary fiber: 12 grams

HUNGARIAN GOULASH

(Serves 4)

This hearty stew traditionally contains meat. I've substituted seitan for the meat and also used eggless noodles, which can be purchased in many supermarkets and natural foods stores today.

8-ounce package seitan, drained and cubed
1 onion, peeled and chopped
2 teaspoons oil
1/2 teaspoon paprika
1 teaspoon caraway seeds
10 cups water
12-ounce package eggless noodles

Sauté seitan, onion, oil, paprika, and caraway seeds in a large frying pan over medium heat for 8 minutes.

Meanwhile, bring water to a boil in a large pot. Reduce heat and cook noodles for 10 minutes until tender. Drain.

Serve seitan mixture over cooked noodles.

Total calories per serving: 329
Fat: 3 grams   Total Fat as % of Daily Value: 5%   Protein: 18 grams   Iron: 4 mg
Carbohydrate: 57 grams   Calcium: 34 mg   Dietary fiber: 2.1 grams

INDIAN CURRY AND RICE
(Serves 4)

Indian food often is spicy and hot. If you dislike green chili, simply eliminate it and enjoy a milder form of this recipe.

1/2 teaspoon mustard seed
1 Tablespoon oil
1 onion, peeled and chopped
1/2 teaspoon garlic powder
1/2 teaspoon turmeric
1/4 teaspoon coriander
1/4 teaspoon cinnamon
1 green chili pepper, finely chopped
Two 8-ounce packages seitan, drained and cubed

Heat mustard seed and oil in a large covered frying pan over medium-high heat until seeds pop. Add remaining ingredients and sauté 8 minutes. Serve with rice below.

2 cups white basmati rice
4 cups water
1/2 teaspoon powdered cloves
1 teaspoon cinnamon
1/2 teaspoon turmeric
Salt and pepper to taste

Cook all the ingredients in a large covered pot over medium heat for 30 minutes.

Total calories per serving: 514
Fat: 4 grams   Total Fat as % of Daily Value: 6%   Protein: 28 grams   Iron: 7 mg
Carbohydrate: 90 grams   Calcium: 60 mg   Dietary fiber: 1.2 grams

ISRAELI BEANS WITH APPLES
(Serves 4)

Traditionally navy beans are used in this recipe; however, any cooked white beans can be used. This recipe calls for apple juice concentrate as a sweetener instead of the more commonly used honey.

4 cups cooked navy or other white beans, drained
4 apples, cored and chopped
1 teaspoon cinnamon
3 Tablespoons wine vinegar
3 Tablespoons apple juice concentrate

Combine all the ingredients in a large pot and simmer over medium-high heat for 10 minutes, stirring occasionally. Serve warm.

Total calories per serving: 314
Fat: 1 gram   Total Fat as % of Daily Value: 2%   Protein: 15 grams   Iron: 4.2 mg
Carbohydrate: 64 grams   Calcium: 133 mg   Dietary fiber: 9.7 grams

LEBANESE GREEN BEAN AND CHICKPEA STEW

(Serves 6)

A touch of cinnamon adds a unique touch to this hearty Lebanese stew.

1 large onion, peeled and finely chopped
2 cloves garlic, peeled and minced
2 teaspoon oil
1 pound green beans, chopped
1 cup water
4 cups pre-cooked chickpeas, drained (two 19-ounce cans)
2 teaspoons cinnamon
1 teaspoon salt
Pepper to taste
3 large ripe tomatoes, chopped

Sauté onion and garlic in oil for 2 minutes in a large pot over medium-high heat. Add string beans and stir-fry 5 minutes longer. Add water, cooked chickpeas, and seasonings. Simmer for 10 minutes. Add tomatoes and simmer 5 minutes longer, stirring occasionally. Serve warm over brown rice or with a baked potato.

Total calories per serving: 247
Fat: 4 grams   Total Fat as % of Daily Value: 6%   Protein: 10 grams   Iron: 3.3 mg
Carbohydrate: 46 grams   Calcium: 98 mg   Dietary fiber: 9 grams

MOROCCAN COUSCOUS AND PUMPKIN

(Serves 4)

Couscous is an extremely fast-cooking grain. Add pumpkin, and you've got yourself an unusual, but delicious meal. For variety, you can also substitute acorn squash for the pumpkin.

1 pound pumpkin, remove seeds, then chopped
1 cup water
1 cup couscous
1 small onion, peeled and minced
1/4 cup slivered almonds
1/4 cup raisins
1 teaspoon cinnamon
1/2 cup maple syrup

Steam pumpkin in water in a covered pot over medium heat for 5 minutes. Add remaining ingredients and simmer in covered pot for 2 minutes. Turn off heat and let covered pot sit for 3 minutes longer. Stir and serve immediately.

Total calories per serving: 338
Fat: 5 grams Total Fat as % of Daily Value: 8% Protein: 7 grams Iron: 2.6 mg
Carbohydrate: 70 grams Calcium: 76 mg Dietary fiber: 3.6 grams

NOODLES AND CABBAGE
(Serves 6)

This inexpensive dish is very easy to prepare. Experiment with different types of cabbage for variety and color.

10 cups water
12-ounce package eggless noodles
3 pounds cabbage, cored and shredded
1 onion, peeled and chopped
2 teaspoons oil
1/4 cup water
1/4 teaspoon paprika
Salt and pepper to taste

Bring water to boil in a large pot. Reduce heat and add noodles. Cook for 10 minutes until noodles are tender. Drain.

Meanwhile, in a separate large frying pan, stir-fry cabbage, onion, oil, water, and seasonings over a medium-high heat for 10 minutes. Add cooked noodles and stir-fry another 3 minutes. Serve warm.

Total calories per serving: 229
Fat: 2 grams Total Fat as % of Daily Value: 3% Protein: 8 grams Iron: 2.6 mg
Carbohydrate: 46 grams   Calcium: 122 mg   Dietary fiber: 9.1 grams

PASSOVER VEGETARIAN KISHKE
(Serves 12)

This vegetarian kishke (stuffing-like mixture) is sure to please guests at your next Passover seder.

4 stalks celery, chopped
2 carrots, grated
2 onions, peeled and minced
2 cups water
1/4 cup oil
4 cups matzo meal
1 Tablespoon paprika
2 teaspoons garlic powder
1/4 teaspoon pepper
1 teaspoon salt

Preheat oven to 350 degrees.

Mix all the ingredients together in a large bowl. Spoon 1/4 of mixture onto a large piece of aluminum foil. Roll mixture in foil into an 8-inch cylinder. Do the same with the remaining mixture to form four 8-inch cylinders. Place cylinders on cookie sheet and bake in a 350-degree oven for 45 minutes. Turn cylinders over and bake 45 minutes longer. Remove foil and serve kishke sliced and warm.

Total calories per serving: 226
Fat:5 grams   Total Fat as % of Daily Value:8%   Protein:5 grams   Iron:0.3 mg
Carbohydrate: 40 grams   Calcium: 13 mg   Dietary fiber: 2.2 grams

POLISH KASHA
WITH MUSHROOMS
(Serves 4)

Experiment with different types of mushrooms when preparing this Polish dish.

1 pound mushrooms, chopped
2 teaspoons oil
2 cups kasha or buckwheat groats
4 cups water
Salt and pepper to taste

Stir-fry mushrooms with oil in a large frying pan over medium-high heat for 5 minutes. Add the kasha or buckwheat groats and stir-fry 2 more minutes.

Next add the water and seasonings. Simmer over medium heat for 20 minutes longer. Stir occasionally to prevent sticking. Serve warm with a baked potato and steamed greens.

Total calories per serving: 309
Fat: 5 grams   Total Fat as % of Daily Value: 8%   Protein: 11 grams   Iron: 3.9 mg
Carbohydrate: 65 grams   Calcium: 41 mg   Dietary fiber: 9.2 grams

POLISH
SPLIT PEA FRITTERS
(Serves 6)

Although split peas take an hour to cook, this recipe is well worth the wait.

2 cups yellow split peas
5 cups water
1 onion, peeled and minced
4 slices whole wheat bread, cubed into small pieces
1 Tablespoon fresh dill or parsley, finely chopped
Salt and pepper to taste
2 Tablespoons oil

Place yellow split peas and water in a pot and simmer over medium heat for 1 hour. Remove pan from the stove and add the remaining ingredients, except for the oil. Mix the ingredients together and form 12 burgers.

Heat oil in a large frying pan over medium-high heat. Fry burgers for 5 minutes, then flip burgers carefully and fry them for 5 minutes longer. (You may have to do this in two batches.) Serve two burgers per person.

Total calories per serving: 256
Fat: 6 grams   Total Fat as % of Daily Value: 9%   Protein: 14 grams   Iron: 3.1 mg
Carbohydrate: 40 grams   Calcium: 35 mg   Dietary fiber: 6.1 grams

RICE, CHICKPEA, AND SPINACH DISH
(Serves 4)

This is a dish eaten often by Jews from Greece.

1 cup brown rice
3-1/2 cups water
1 large onion, peeled and chopped
2 teaspoons oil
2 cups pre-cooked chickpeas, drained (19-ounce can)
1/2 pound fresh spinach, rinsed and chopped
Salt and pepper to taste

Cook rice with water in a large pot over medium-high heat for 35 minutes or until tender. While the rice is cooking, sauté onion with oil in a large frying pan over medium-high heat for 2 minutes. Add chickpeas and stir-fry 3 minutes longer. Next add the spinach and seasonings. Stir-fry another 3 minutes.

Add the cooked rice to the chickpea/spinach mixture. Serve warm.

Total calories per serving: 336
Fat: 5 grams   Total Fat as % of Daily Value: 8%   Protein: 11 grams   Iron: 4 mg
Carbohydrate: 64 grams   Calcium: 109 mg   Dietary fiber: 8.6 grams

ROMANIAN MUSHROOM PAPRIKASH
(Serves 6)

My friend Mircea, who was raised as a child in Romania, taught me how to make this hearty dish. He recommends that the dish be served with dilled cucumbers or sour pickles.

1 pound button mushrooms or larger mushrooms,
    quartered
1 onion, peeled and finely chopped
2 Tablespoons oil
1 cup fresh parsley, finely chopped
2 cloves garlic, minced
1 Tablespoon paprika
1 Tablespoon unbleached white flour
Salt and pepper to taste
2 pounds white potatoes, peeled and chopped
1 pound elbow macaroni

Stir-fry mushrooms and onions with oil in a large frying pan over medium-high heat for 5 minutes. Add parsley, garlic, paprika, flour, salt and pepper to taste, and potatoes. Cover the ingredients with water and simmer 15 minutes in covered pan until potatoes are tender. Stir occasionally to prevent sticking.

Meanwhile, cook macaroni in water until tender. Drain and add to the mushroom/potato mixture. Serve warm.

Total calories per serving: 414
Fat: 6 grams   Total Fat as % of Daily Value: 9%   Protein:11 grams   Iron: 4.1 mg
Carbohydrate: 80 grams   Calcium: 52 mg   Dietary fiber: 7.3 grams

RUSSIAN BLINI
(Serves 4)

Blini are pancakes that Russian Jews traditionally serve as a main dish. These pancakes are delicious when served with fruit compote (see page 175) or baked fruit (see page 174).

2 teaspoons active dry yeast
1 cup warm water
1 cup soy milk
2 bananas, peeled and mashed
1/2 cup whole wheat pastry flour
1-1/4 cups buckwheat flour
1-1/2 teaspoons oil

Dissolve yeast in water in a large bowl. Add remaining ingredients, except oil, and mix well. Allow mixture to sit in warm place for 1 hour.

Heat oil on large griddle over medium heat. Pour 1/4 of batter at a time onto the griddle to make 4 pancakes. Cook 5 minutes. Flip pancakes and cook another 4 minutes. Serve warm.

Total calories per serving: 269
Fat: 5 grams   Total Fat as % of Daily Value: 8 %   Protein: 10 grams   Iron: 3.1 mg
Carbohydrate: 51 grams   Calcium: 45 mg   Dietary fiber: 8 grams

RUSSIAN CHICKPEA BAKE
(Serves 6)

This simple Russian dish traditionally contains honey. I use maple syrup instead.

**3-1/2 cups pre-cooked chickpeas, drained (two 15-
    ounce cans)**
1/4 cup maple syrup
1 teaspoon cinnamon

Preheat oven to 350 degrees.
   Mix all the ingredients together in a bowl. Pour into a small loaf pan and bake at 350 degrees for 45 minutes, stirring every 15 minutes. Serve warm.

Total calories per serving: 200
Fat:2 grams   Total Fat as % of Daily Value:3%   Protein:7 grams   Iron:1.9 mg
Carbohydrate: 40 grams   Calcium: 47 mg   Dietary fiber: 5 grams

RUSSIAN MUSHROOM CUTLETS
(Serves 6)

Mushrooms are quite popular in Russia. Try different varieties of mushrooms available in the marketplace today.

3 cups brown rice
10 cups water
1 pound mushrooms, chopped
1/4 cup whole wheat pastry flour
Salt and pepper to taste
1 Tablespoon oil

Cook rice in water until done. Add chopped mushrooms to cooked rice and mix well. Blend half of the mixture in a food processor for 3 minutes and pour into a large bowl. Repeat with the other half of mixture.

Add flour and seasonings. Mix well and form 12 cutlets. Fry cutlets in oiled pan for 10 minutes. Flip over and continue frying for 10 minutes longer. Top with gravy (recipe follows on page 114).

Total calories per serving: 404
Fat: 4 grams   Total Fat as % of Daily Value: 6%   Protein:10 grams   Iron: 2.6 mg
Carbohydrate: 82 grams   Calcium: 41 mg   Dietary fiber: 5.8 grams

GRAVY
(Serves 6)

This delicious gravy goes perfectly with the Russian Mushroom Cutlets on page 113.

2 teaspoons oil
1/2 pound mushrooms, thinly sliced
1 onion, peeled and finely chopped
2 Tablespoons whole wheat pastry flour
1 cup water
Salt and pepper to taste

Sauté mushrooms, onion, and oil in a frying pan for 3 minutes over medium-high heat. Add remaining ingredients and stir constantly over medium heat for about 2 minutes until gravy thickens. Serve gravy over mushroom cutlets.

Total calories per serving: 37
Fat: 2 grams   Total Fat as % of Daily Value: 3%   Protein: 1 gram   Iron: .6 mg
Carbohydrate: 5 grams   Calcium: 7 mg   Dietary fiber: 1.5 grams

RUSSIAN NOODLES WITH CHERRIES

(Serves 4)

Traditionally sour cherries and sugar are used to prepare this dish. Instead, I use sweet cherries and fruit juice. You can also substitute other fruit such as chopped plums or peaches.

12-ounce package eggless noodles
10 cups water
1 pound sweet cherries, pitted and chopped in half
1/2 cup apple juice
2 Tablespoons cornstarch
1/2 cup water

Cook noodles in 10 cups boiling water for 8 minutes until done. Drain noodles.

Meanwhile, in separate small pot heat cherries with juice over medium heat for 5 minutes. Dissolve cornstarch in 1/2 cup water and add to cooking cherries. Simmer 1 minute longer, stirring occasionally. Add cooked cherries to cooked noodles and serve warm.

Total calories per serving: 342
Fat: 2 grams   Total Fat as % of Daily Value: 3%   Protein: 8 grams   Iron: 2.4 mg
Carbohydrate: 74 grams   Calcium: 36 mg   Dietary fiber: 3 grams

RUSSIAN POTATO AND MUSHROOM CROQUETTES

(Serves 5)

Enjoy these delicious croquettes during Passover, as well as the rest of the year.

1-1/2 pounds potatoes, peeled and chopped
5 cups water
1 onion, peeled and chopped
1/4 pound mushrooms
1 teaspoon oil
1 Tablespoon water
Salt and pepper to taste
1 cup matzo meal
1 Tablespoon oil

Boil potatoes in water until tender. Drain and mash potatoes.

In a separate pan sauté onion and mushrooms in oil and water over medium-high heat for 3 minutes. Mix the mashed potatoes, sautéed onion and mushrooms, seasonings, and matzo meal together in a large bowl. Form 10 burgers.

Heat oil in a large frying pan over medium-high heat. Fry burgers for 8 minutes, flip over and continue frying for another 8 minutes. Serve two burgers per person.

Total calories per serving: 265
Fat: 4 grams   Total Fat as % of Daily Value: 6%   Protein: 6 grams   Iron: 0.8 mg
Carbohydrate: 52 grams   Calcium: 17 mg   Dietary fiber: 4.3 grams

SEITAN AND BULGUR STEW

(Serves 4)

Seitan is an excellent alternative to beef in a stew.

1 onion, peeled and finely chopped
2 teaspoons oil
1-1/2 cups bulgur
3 cups vegetable broth
8-ounce package of seitan, drained
Salt and pepper to taste

Sauté onion with oil in a large pot for 2 minutes. Add bulgur and broth. Cover pot and simmer over medium heat for 15 minutes. Stir occasionally to prevent sticking.

While bulgur is cooking, chop seitan into bite-size pieces. Add seitan and seasonings to the pot. Continue heating uncovered for another 5 minutes. Serve stew warm.

Total calories per serving: 323
Fat: 4 grams   Total Fat as % of Daily Value: 6%   Protein: 20 grams   Iron: 3.8 mg
Carbohydrate: 54 grams   Calcium: 46 mg   Dietary fiber: 6 grams

SEITAN AND ONIONS OVER MASHED POTATOES

(Serves 3)

This is an excellent alternative to onions with beef.

5 potatoes, peeled and chopped
5 cups water
1 onion, peeled and finely chopped
2 teaspoons oil
Salt and pepper to taste
8-ounce package of seitan, drained and chopped into
    bite-size pieces

Place potatoes and water in a large pot and simmer over medium heat until potatoes are tender (about 30 minutes). Drain and mash potatoes.

While potatoes are cooking, sauté onion in oil for 2 minutes. Add seitan and seasonings. Stir-fry 5 minutes longer. Serve seitan and onions over mashed potatoes.

Total calories per serving: 322
Fat: 3 grams   Total Fat as % of Daily Value: 5%   Protein: 18 grams   Iron: 3.5 mg
Carbohydrate: 56 grams   Calcium: 40 mg   Dietary fiber: 5 grams

SPINACH PIES

(Serves 8)

Spinach pies are a lot of fun to eat. Here I've substituted crumbled tofu for feta cheese.

Two 10-ounce packages frozen chopped spinach, cooked
1 teaspoon oil
1 small onion, peeled and chopped finely
1/2 pound soft tofu, crumbled
1/2 teaspoon salt
8 sheets of Phyllo dough
1 Tablespoon margarine

Cook spinach for 5 minutes in water and drain.

In separate large pan, sauté onion and tofu in oil with salt for 2 minutes over medium-high heat. Add cooked spinach and sauté 1 minute longer.

Preheat oven to 375 degrees. Meanwhile melt margarine in a small pan over low heat.

Remove 4 sheets of phyllo dough. Cut into 4 equal rectangles. Place approximately 4 Tablespoons of mixture in center of each rectangle. Fold ends in. Repeat this procedure one more time to make a total of 8 spinach pies.

Place pies on a lightly oiled cookie sheet. Brush pies on top with melted margarine. Bake for 35 minutes at 375 degrees until brown on top. Serve warm.

Total calories per serving: 122
Fat:4 grams   Total Fat as % of Daily Value:6%   Protein:7 grams   Iron:3.6 mg
Carbohydrates: 18 grams   Calcium:161 mg   Dietary fiber: 2.6 grams

SYRIAN CHICKPEA AND BULGUR STEW

(Serves 4)

A combination of chickpeas and bulgur make this a hearty stew sure to fill up hungry guests.

1 cup bulgur
1-1/2 cups cooked chickpeas, drained (15-ounce can)
1 small onion, peeled and finely chopped
4 cups water
2 ripe tomatoes, chopped
Salt and pepper to taste

Cook bulgur, chickpeas, and onion with water in a large pot over medium heat for 15 minutes. Stir occasionally. Add tomatoes and seasonings and continue heating for 5 minutes longer. Serve warm with steamed greens.

Total calories per serving: 266
Fat: 2 grams   Total Fat as % of Daily Value: 3%   Protein: 10 grams   Iron: 2.7 mg
Carbohydrate: 54 grams   Calcium: 55 mg   Dietary fiber: 8.2 grams

TURKISH BLACK-EYED PEAS OVER RICE

(Serves 5)

This delicious dish creatively uses black-eyed peas.

2 cups brown rice
5 cups water
2 large onions, peeled and finely chopped
1 Tablespoon oil
Two 10-ounce boxes frozen black-eyed peas
3 cups water
1 cup lemon juice
6 ripe tomatoes, chopped
Salt and pepper to taste

Cook rice in water in a large pot until done.

Meanwhile, stir-fry onions in oil for 2 minutes in a large pot. Add black-eyed peas, water, and lemon juice. Cover pot and simmer for 30 minutes, stirring occasionally. Add tomatoes and seasonings. Simmer 10 minutes longer, stirring occasionally. Serve hot over cooked rice.

Total calories per serving: 498
Fat: 5 grams   Total Fat as % of Daily Value: 8%   Protein: 18 grams   Iron: 5.5 mg
Carbohydrate: 97 grams   Calcium: 87 mg   Dietary fiber: 12.5 grams

UKRAINIAN KASHA VARNISHKES
(Serves 6)

Kasha is cracked buckwheat and is often called buckwheat groats in the United States. Varnishkes are noodles.

2 cups kasha or buckwheat groats
1 large onion, peeled and finely chopped
2 teaspoons oil
4 cups water
12-ounce package of eggless noodles
10 cups water
Salt and pepper to taste

Sauté kasha or buckwheat groats and onion with oil in a large frying pan over medium-high heat for 3 minutes. Add 4 cups water and simmer covered for 20 minutes.

Meanwhile, in a separate pot, cook noodles in 10 cups water until tender. Drain noodles and add to kasha mixture along with the seasonings. Serve warm.

Total calories per serving: 327
Fat: 4 grams Total Fat as % of Daily Value:6% Protein: 10 grams Iron: 2.7 mg
Carbohydrate: 66 grams   Calcium: 39 mg   Dietary fiber: 5.3 grams

VEGETARIAN CHOLENT
(Serves 8)

Almost every Jewish household has served cholent, a slow-cooking stew. This is a simple, quicker vegetarian version.

2-1/2 pounds sweet potatoes, peeled and cubed
4 cups water
1-1/2 pounds white potatoes, peeled and cubed
1 pound carrots, peeled and chopped
2 cups pre-cooked chickpeas, drained (19-ounce can)
2 teaspoons cinnamon
1/2 teaspoon coriander
2 ripe tomatoes, chopped

Cook sweet potatoes with water in a large pot over medium-high heat for 20 minutes. Add white potatoes and carrots and cook 20 minutes longer. Next add the chickpeas and continue cooking for 10 minutes. Finally, add the spices and tomatoes. Simmer 10 minutes longer and serve warm.

Total calories per serving: 321
Fat: 1 gram   Total Fat as % of Daily Value: 2%   Protein: 8 grams   Iron: 2.1 mg
Carbohydrate: 72 grams   Calcium: 83 mg   Dietary fiber: 9.8 grams

YEMENITE GREEN BEAN STEW
(Serves 5)

This unique green bean dish has a wonderful flavor.

1-1/2 cups brown rice
5 cups water
1 large onion, peeled and finely chopped
2 teaspoons oil
1-1/2 pounds green beans, chopped
2 teaspoons coriander
Salt and pepper to taste
One 29-ounce can tomato puree

Cook brown rice and water in a pot over medium heat for 45 minutes until tender.

In a separate pan, stir-fry onion in oil over medium heat for 2 minutes. Add green beans and coriander and stir-fry 10 minutes longer. Add salt, pepper, and tomato puree. Simmer 10 minutes. Stir in cooked rice and serve warm.

Total calories per serving: 343
Fat: 3 grams   Total Fat as % of Daily Value: 5%   Protein: 10 grams   Iron: 3.8 mg
Carbohydrates: 73 grams   Calcium: 116 mg   Dietary fiber: 9.7 grams

STUFFED VEGETABLES

ARMENIAN STUFFED EGGPLANT
(Serves 4)

Throughout the world, Jews of different backgrounds stuff vegetables in creative ways to serve either as a side or main dish. Here, eggplant is filled with a bulgur (cracked wheat) stuffing containing a touch of mint.

2 medium eggplants
2 cups water
1 small onion, peeled and finely chopped
1 pound mushrooms, finely chopped
2 teaspoons oil
1/4 cup bulgur
1-3/4 cups vegetable broth
1 Tablespoon dried mint
Salt and pepper to taste

Steam whole eggplants over water in a large covered pot for 15 minutes. Remove from pot and slice in half lengthwise. Scoop out eggplant pulp from each half, leaving 1/4-inch thick shell.

Stir-fry eggplant pulp, onion, and mushrooms with oil in a large (preferably non-stick) frying pan over medium heat for 10 minutes. Add bulgur, broth, mint, and seasonings. Simmer covered for 20 minutes longer, stirring occasionally.

Preheat oven to 375 degrees. Meanwhile, stuff cooked mixture into eggplant shells. Place stuffed eggplants on a lightly oiled baking pan and bake at 375 degrees for 30 minutes. Serve warm.

Total calories per serving: 174
Fat: 4 grams   Total Fat as % of Daily Value: 6%   Protein: 8 grams   Iron: 3.8 mg
Carbohydrates: 32 grams   Calcium: 53 mg   Dietary fiber: 6.7 grams

BARLEY
STUFFED LETTUCE
(Serves 4 -- 3 leaves per person)

Many Americans make stuffed cabbage, but few ever think of stuffing lettuce leaves. Try different varieties of lettuce as the jacket and rice or cous cous in place of the barley as the filling. Also, experiment with different juices.

1-1/2 cups barley
3 cups orange juice
2 cups water
2 teaspoons cinnamon
1 cup raisins
1 head of romaine lettuce or other large leaf lettuce
2 cups tomato sauce

Cook barley with juice, water, cinnamon, and raisins in a large covered pot over medium-low heat for 1 hour.

Preheat oven to 350 degrees. Separate 12 lettuce leaves and rinse well. Stuff each leaf with about 3 Tablespoons cooked barley mixture. Fold ends of leaves under. Pour tomato sauce into a baking pan. Lay stuffed leaves in pan with folded ends down. Bake 15 minutes at 350 degrees. Serve warm.

Total calories per serving: 521
Fat: 1 gram   Total Fat as % of Daily Value: 2%   Protein: 13 grams   Iron: 4.2 mg
Carbohydrates: 119 grams   Calcium: 82 mg   Dietary fiber: 12.9 grams

FRUIT STUFFED GREEN PEPPERS
(Serves 8)

This is a delicious stuffed pepper recipe. Experiment with different grains such as barley and couscous instead of the brown rice. You can also use other varieties of dried fruit in place of the raisins, as well as different color bell peppers.

3/4 cup brown rice
2 cups water
8 large green peppers
2 teaspoons oil
2 onions, peeled and finely chopped
2 cloves garlic, peeled and minced
3 Tablespoons sunflower seeds
2 Tablespoons sesame seeds
1/4 cup unbleached white flour
1 apple, cored and finely chopped
3 Tablespoons raisins
1/2 cup fruit juice
1-1/2 Tablespoons tamari or soy sauce

Cook rice in water in a pot over medium heat for 50 minutes or until done.

Meanwhile, slice off the tops of each pepper and scoop out seeds. Set the peppers aside.

Sauté oil, onions, garlic, sunflower and sesame seeds, and flour in a large frying pan over medium heat for 3 minutes. Add apple, raisins, juice, and tamari. Cover pan and lower heat. Simmer for 15 minutes. Combine mixture with cooked rice. Stuff mixture into peppers.

Preheat oven to 375 degrees. Set peppers in a lightly oiled baking dish. Bake at 375 degrees for 30 minutes. Serve warm.

Total calories per serving: 176
Fat: 5 grams   Total Fat as % of Daily Value: 8%   Protein: 4 grams   Iron: 2.5 mg
Carbohydrates: 31 grams   Calcium: 47 mg   Dietary fiber: 3.8 grams

ISRAELI STUFFED GRAPE LEAVES

(Serves 9 -- 6 per person)

Grape leaves can be found in many supermarkets and natural food stores today. This dish is wonderful to serve at a party, along with hummus, baba ghanoush, and tabouli.

16-ounce jar grape leaves in brine
4 cups boiling water
1 onion, peeled and finely chopped
2 teaspoons oil
1-1/2 cups brown rice
4 cups water
2 cloves garlic, peeled and minced
3 Tablespoons lemon juice
1/4 cup parsley, finely chopped
2 teaspoons dried mint
1 teaspoon allspice
1/2 cup pine nuts (optional), chopped
1/2 teaspoon salt

Remove grape leaves from jar and place in a large bowl. Pour boiling water over grape leaves and allow to sit 20 minutes. Drain and rinse leaves twice with cold water. Set aside.

Stir-fry onion with oil in a large frying pan over medium heat for 2 minutes. Add remaining ingredients. Bring to a boil, then simmer for 45 minutes until rice is done.

Preheat oven to 350 degrees. Stuff grape leaves with 1 Tablespoon of rice mixture per leaf. Fold ends of leaves under and place with folded ends down on a lightly oiled pan. Sprinkle top of leaves with a little water. Bake at 350 degrees for 20 minutes. Serve warm.

Total calories per serving: 125
Fat: 2 grams   Total Fat as % of Daily Value: 3%   Protein: 3 grams   Iron: 1.9 mg
Carbohydrates: 23 grams   Calcium: 131 mg   Dietary fiber: 3.3 grams

POLISH STUFFED CABBAGE
(Serves 6 -- 2 per person)

My Polish grandmother often served me stuffed cabbage as a child. In this variation of her recipe, I've used barley instead of rice.

1 cup barley
4-1/2 cups water
1 cup raisins
1 teaspoon cinnamon
1 cabbage (about 1-1/2 pounds)
2 cups water
3 cups tomato sauce

Cook barley in water in a large covered pot over medium heat for 40 minutes. Add raisins and cinnamon and continue cooking for another 10 minutes, stirring occasionally.

While the barley is cooking, remove cabbage core. Steam cabbage over 2 cups water in a large pot over medium heat for 10 minutes. Remove from pot and allow to cool for a few minutes. Carefully remove 12 outer cabbage leaves.

Preheat oven to 375 degrees. Place 1/12th of mixture in center of each cabbage leaf. Fold ends of leaves in. Place cabbage with folded part under on a lightly oiled pan. Pour sauce over stuffed cabbage. Bake 25 minutes. Serve warm.

Total calories per serving: 266
Fat: 1 gram   Total Fat as % of Daily Value: 2%   Protein: 8 grams   Iron: 3 mg
Carbohydrates: 62 grams   Calcium: 91 mg   Dietary fiber: 12.1 grams

STUFFED CABBAGE
(Serves 6 -- 2 per person)

Here's a unique stuffed cabbage recipe using tofu and sweetened with apple juice and raisins. Children will enjoy this dish.

1 cabbage (about 1-1/2 pounds)
2 cups water
1-1/2 pounds tofu, crumbled
1/2 cup water
1 cup raisins
6 ounce can tomato paste
1 teaspoon cinnamon
2 cups apple juice

Remove cabbage core. Steam cabbage over 2 cups water in a large pot over medium heat for 10 minutes. Remove from pot and allow to cool for a few minutes. Carefully remove 12 outer cabbage leaves.

Preheat oven to 375 degrees. Meanwhile, mix together the remaining ingredients, except the juice, and place 1/12th of the mixture in the center of each cabbage leaf. Fold ends of leaves in and place the stuffed cabbage with the folded ends down in a baking pan. Pour apple juice in pan and bake cabbage at 375 degrees for 30 minutes. Serve warm.

Total calories per serving: 263
Fat: 6 grams   Total Fat as % of Daily Value: 9%   Protein: 13 grams   Iron: 8.6 mg
Carbohydrates: 46 grams   Calcium: 204 mg   Dietary fiber: 7.5 grams

STUFFED KOHLRABI
(Serves 4 -- 2 large or 3 small per person)

This recipe was adapted from one given to me by a Romanian friend. Few Americans are familiar with kohlrabi, therefore you will find this to be a delicious, unique dish. Serve with dill sauce (recipe on page 135).

12 small or 8 large kohlrabi
2 teaspoons oil
1/4 pound mushrooms, finely chopped
1/2 small onion, peeled and grated
1 clove garlic, peeled and minced
1 carrot, peeled and finely grated
1/4 cup parsley, finely chopped
Salt and pepper to taste
1/4 teaspoon paprika
1/4 teaspoon thyme
2 Tablespoons pumpkin or sunflower seeds (optional)
1 cup pre-cooked brown rice
2 Tablespoons whole wheat pastry flour

Preheat oven to 375 degrees.

Remove leaves and stems from kohlrabi and peel. Scoop out flesh from each kohlrabi, leaving 1/2-inch shell. Finely chop kohlrabi flesh and sauté with onion, garlic, carrot, parsley, seasonings, and seeds in oil in a large frying pan over medium-high heat for 5 minutes. Add cooked rice and flour. Mix well. Stuff mixture into kohlrabi shells. Bake at 375 degrees for 45 minutes. Dill sauce recipe follows.

Total calories per serving: 151
Fat: 3 grams   Total Fat as % of Daily Value: 5%   Protein: 6 grams   Iron: 1.8 mg
Carbohydrates: 29 grams   Calcium: 60 mg   Dietary fiber: 4.4 grams

DILL SAUCE
(Serves 4)

Serve this light but pungent sauce over stuffed kohlrabi (see recipe on page 134). You can also pour it over any steamed vegetables or greens, and use it as a sandwich spread.

1 clove garlic, peeled and minced
1/4 cup fresh dill, finely chopped
1 Tablespoon fresh parsley, finely chopped
1 shallot, peeled and grated or 2 scallions, finely
    chopped
1 teaspoon oil
1 Tablespoon unbleached white flour
1/2 cup vegetable broth
1 Tablespoon lemon juice
Salt and pepper to taste

Sauté garlic, dill, parsley, and shallot with oil in a large frying pan over medium-high heat for 3 minutes. Add flour, broth, lemon juice, and seasonings. Stir until mixture thickens. Remove from heat and serve over stuffed kohlrabi.

Total calories per serving: 25
Fat: 1 gram   Total Fat as % of Daily Value: 2%   Protein: 1 gram   Iron: 0.5 mg
Carbohydrates: 3 grams   Calcium: 14 mg   Dietary fiber: 0.5 grams

STUFFED MUSHROOMS

(Serves 5 -- 3 large or 4 medium per person)

This is another great recipe to prepare for a party. Bake them shortly before you are going to serve them.

1/2 cup lentils
1 cup water
1 scallion, chopped finely
1 small onion, peeled and finely chopped
2 teaspoons oil
2 Tablespoons water
Dash of pepper to taste
20 medium mushrooms or 15 large mushrooms

Cook lentils in water in a small pot over medium heat for 55 minutes. Remove from heat and mash.

Sauté scallion and onion with oil and water in a frying pan over medium heat for 3 minutes. Add cooked lentils and pepper. Sauté another 3 minutes. Remove from heat.

Preheat oven to 450 degrees. Meanwhile, take caps off mushrooms. Discard stems. Stuff mushroom caps with lentil mixture. Place mushrooms on a lightly oiled pan and bake at 450 degrees for 12 minutes. Serve warm.

Total calories per serving: 93
Fat:2 grams   Total Fat as % of Daily Value: 3%   Protein: 6 grams   Iron: 2.5 mg
Carbohydrates: 14 grams   Calcium: 18 mg   Dietary fiber: 4 grams

STUFFED TOMATOES
(Serves 6)

This is a great recipe to prepare during the summer when you don't know what to do with all the tomatoes you may have grown in your backyard garden.

6 medium ripe tomatoes
2/3 cup bulgur (cracked wheat)
1-1/2 cups water
1 teaspoon dried mint
1/2 teaspoon cinnamon

Scoop out pulp from one tomato and set that pulp aside. Scoop out the pulp from the remaining 5 tomatoes and place the pulp in a pot. Add the remaining ingredients to the pot and heat the ingredients over a medium heat for 25 minutes.

Stuff the tomatoes with the bulgur mixture and sprinkle the tomato pulp you had set aside over the tomatoes. Place the stuffed tomatoes in a baking dish. Pour 1 cup of water into the bottom of the dish. Broil 12 minutes in an oven. Serve warm.

Total calories per serving: 80
Fat: 1 gram   Total Fat as % of Daily Value: 2%   Protein: 3 grams   Iron: 1 mg
Carbohydrates: 17 grams   Calcium: 15 mg   Dietary fiber: 3.4 grams

SIDE DISHES

BAKED CARROTS
(Serves 6)

This is a sweet vegetable side dish that young children will especially enjoy.

2 pounds carrots peeled and cut into thin strips
2 cups orange juice
1 onion, peeled and finely chopped
1 teaspoon cinnamon

Preheat oven to 375 degrees.

Mix all the ingredients together in a large bowl. Pour into a casserole dish and cover. Bake on low oven shelf at 375 degrees for 90 minutes or until carrots are tender. Serve warm.

Total calories per serving: 108
Fat: <1 gram   Total Fat as % of Daily Value: <1%   Protein: 2 grams   Iron: 0.9 mg
Carbohydrates: 26 grams   Calcium: 53 mg   Dietary fiber: 5.3 grams

BROCCOLI LATKES
(Serves 5)

Many people have tried potato latkes (pancakes) before. This latke recipe adds broccoli and a touch of celery seed to create a unique combination.

1 pound broccoli, chopped into small pieces
2 pounds potatoes, scrubbed and cubed into small
   pieces
1 onion, peeled and finely chopped
3 cups water
1/2 teaspoon celery seed
Salt and pepper to taste
1 Tablespoon oil

Cook all the ingredients (except the oil) in a large covered pot over medium heat for 20 minutes. Drain mixture. Mash ingredients together.

Heat oil in large non-stick frying pan over medium heat. Form 10 pancakes. Fry 8 minutes on one side. Flip and fry for another 5 minutes on the other side. Serve warm.

Total calories per serving: 211
Fat: 3 grams   Total Fat as % of Daily Value: 5%   Protein: 6 grams   Iron: 1.2 mg
Carbohydrates: 43 grams   Calcium: 66 mg   Dietary fiber: 6.9 grams

BROCCOLI AND LEMON SAUCE

(Serves 5)

Make sure you try this quick and easy side dish. The lemon sauce can also be used on top of other steamed vegetables such as green beans, yellow squash, or cauliflower.

2 pounds broccoli, chopped
1 cup water
Juice of 2 fresh lemons
1/4 cup water
1 Tablespoon cornstarch or potato starch for Passover

Steam broccoli over water in a large pot for several minutes until tender.

In a separate pot over medium heat constantly stir lemon juice, water, and cornstarch until the sauce thickens (about 2 minutes). Serve sauce over steamed broccoli while warm.

Total calories per serving: 64
Fat: 0 grams   Total Fat as % of Daily Value: 0%   Protein: 6 grams   Iron: 1.3 mg
Carbohydrates: 14 grams   Calcium: 100 mg   Dietary fiber: 6.6 grams

BULGUR PILAF
(Serves 6)

This hardy Middle Eastern dish combines bulgur (cracked wheat) with several spices, dried fruit, and a small amount of nuts. Experiment with different types of dried fruit and nuts.

1 large onion, peeled and finely chopped
2 teaspoons oil
2 cups bulgur (cracked wheat)
5 cups water
1 teaspoon coriander
1 teaspoon cumin
1 teaspoon cinnamon
1/4 cup slivered almonds
1 cup dried apricots, chopped
1 cup raisins
Salt and pepper to taste

Stir-fry onion with oil in a large pot for 3 minutes. Add remaining ingredients, cover pot, and cook over medium heat for 15 minutes, stirring occasionally. Remove pot from stove and allow it to sit covered 5 minutes. Mix ingredients well, pour into a serving dish, and serve while still warm.

Total calories per serving: 374
Fat:5 grams   Total Fat as % of Daily Value:8%   Protein:10 grams   Iron:3.3 mg
Carbohydrates: 77 grams   Calcium:65 mg   Dietary fiber: 9.7 grams

CABBAGE SAUTÉ
(Serves 6)

If you're ever in a rush, this is a quick and easy side dish that friends and family will certainly enjoy. Try different varieties of cabbage.

Small head of cabbage, cored and chopped into bite-size pieces
1 onion, peeled and finely chopped
1/3 cup water
2 teaspoons oil
3 tomatoes, chopped
1/4 teaspoon garlic powder
Salt to taste
2 Tablespoons lemon juice

Sauté cabbage and onion with water and oil in a large frying pan over medium-high heat for 5 minutes. Lower heat and add the remaining ingredients and continue sautéing for 5 more minutes. Serve warm.

Total calories per serving: 49
Fat: 2 grams   Total Fat as % of Daily Value: 3%   Protein: 2 grams   Iron: 0.8 mg
Carbohydrates: 8 grams   Calcium: 42 mg   Dietary fiber: 3.5 grams

CARROT AND CABBAGE SAUTÉ

(Serves 6)

By adding a touch of ginger powder and lemon juice, this quick and easy dish is absolutely delicious. It can be served during Passover.

1/2 medium cabbage, shredded
1 pound carrots, peeled and grated
2 cloves garlic, peeled and minced
1/2 teaspoon ginger powder
Salt and pepper to taste
2 teaspoons oil
1 Tablespoon lemon juice

Sauté all the ingredients (except the lemon juice) together in a large frying pan over medium-high heat for 5 minutes. Add the lemon juice and continue sautéing for 2 more minutes. Serve warm.

Total calories per serving: 59
Fat: 2 grams   Total Fat as % of Daily Value: 3%   Protein: 1 gram   Iron: 0.7 mg
Carbohydrates: 11 grams   Calcium: 45 mg   Dietary fiber: 4.1 grams

EASY COUSCOUS DISH
(Serves 4)

This is a very simple side dish made out of couscous, a quick- cooking grain.

Small onion, peeled and finely chopped
1 teaspoon oil
Salt and pepper to taste
1 cup couscous
2 cups vegetable broth (recipe on page 70)

Sauté onion in oil in a large pot over medium heat for 2 minutes. Add remaining ingredients and simmer for 5 minutes longer, stirring occasionally. Remove pot from stove and allow mixture to sit covered for 5 minutes. Stir before serving warm.

Total calories per serving: 139
Fat: 2 grams   Total Fat as % of Daily Value:3%   Protein: 5 grams   Iron: 0.4 mg
Carbohydrates: 26 grams   Calcium: 15 mg   Dietary fiber: 0.2 grams

GREEK CHICKPEAS AND SPINACH
(Serves 6)

Enjoy this typical quick and easy Greek recipe. Serve with rice.

1 large onion, peeled and finely chopped
2 teaspoons oil
2 cups precooked chickpeas (or a 19-ounce can
    garbanzo beans), drained
2 Tablespoons fresh dill, finely chopped
1/2 pound fresh spinach, rinsed and chopped into bite-
    size pieces
2 Tablespoons lemon juice
Salt to taste

Sauté onion in oil in a large frying pan over medium heat for 2 minutes. Add cooked chickpeas and dill. Stir-fry for 5 minutes. Add spinach, lemon juice, and seasonings. Cook another 5 minutes, stirring occasionally. Serve warm.

Total calories per serving: 125
Fat: 3 grams   Total Fat as % of Daily Value: 5%   Protein: 5 grams   Iron: 2.2 mg
Carbohydrates: 21 grams   Calcium: 69 mg   Dietary fiber: 4.7 grams

GREEK RICE WITH CHICKPEAS

(Serves 6)

This Greek recipe combines brown rice with chickpeas, fresh parsley, and lemon juice. You can also substitute other cooked beans including navy or kidney beans.

1 cup brown rice
1 onion, peeled and finely chopped
3-1/2 cups water
1-1/2 cups precooked chickpeas (or a 15-ounce can garbanzo beans), drained
1/4 cup fresh parsley, finely chopped
2 Tablespoons lemon juice
Salt to taste

Cook rice and onion in water in a large covered pot over medium heat for 45 minutes. Add cooked chickpeas, parsley, lemon juice, and salt. Cook another 10 minutes, stirring occasionally. Serve warm.

Total calories per serving: 179
Fat: 2 grams   Total Fat as % of Daily Value:3%   Protein: 5 grams   Iron: 1.5 mg
Carbohydrates: 37 grams   Calcium:32 mg   Dietary fiber: 3.6 grams

GREEK RICE WITH SPINACH

(Serves 6)

Greek Jews often use lemon juice and fresh dill to prepare dishes.
Enjoy this pleasant combination of brown rice and spinach.

2 cups brown rice
6 cups water
1 large onion, peeled and finely chopped
2 teaspoons oil
1/2 pound fresh spinach, rinsed and chopped into bite-
**   size pieces**
1/2 cup fresh dill, finely chopped
2 Tablespoons lemon juice

Cook rice in water in a large covered pot over medium heat for 45 minutes or until rice is done.

Meanwhile, in a separate frying pan, sauté onion in oil for 3 minutes. Add spinach, dill, and lemon juice. Stir-fry for 3 minutes longer. Add cooked rice. Mix well before serving warm.

Total calories per serving: 230
Fat: 3 grams   Total Fat as % of Daily Value: 5%   Protein: 6 grams   Iron: 2.1 mg
Carbohydrates: 46 grams   Calcium: 54 mg   Dietary fiber: 4 grams

ISRAELI SWEET VEGETABLES
(Serves 4)

This is a quick and easy, sweet side dish. Experiment with different combinations of chopped vegetables.

1/2 pound mixed fresh vegetables, (carrots, zucchini, etc.), peeled and chopped
1 cup orange juice
2 teaspoons caraway seeds

Place ingredients in a small covered pot and simmer over medium-low heat for 20 minutes. Serve warm.

Total calories per serving: 46
Fat: <1 gram   Total Fat as % of Daily Value: <1%   Protein: 1 gram   Iron: 0.3 mg
Carbohydrates: 11 grams   Calcium: 19 mg   Dietary fiber: 1.5 grams

ITALIAN SAUTÉED CHICORY
(Serves 6)

This quick and easy dish is traditionally made with chicory; however, you can certainly substitute other greens including kale, collards, beet greens, etc.

1 pound chicory, rinsed and torn into 3-inch pieces
1 cup water
1 teaspoon oil
1 teaspoon garlic powder
1/4 teaspoon salt, tamari, or soy sauce

Heat chicory with water in a covered pot over medium heat for 3 minutes. Remove from heat, stir twice, then rinse cooked chicory. (This eliminates much of what seems like a bitter taste to many people.)

Sauté rinsed, cooked greens in oil with garlic powder and salt over medium heat for 2 minutes. Serve warm.

Total calories per serving: 18
Fat: 1 gram   Total Fat as % of Daily Value: 2%   Protein: 1 gram   Iron: 0.4 mg
Carbohydrates: 2 grams   Calcium: 14 mg   Dietary fiber: 0.6 grams

KASHA AND ONION KNISHES

(Serves 4 -- 2 each)

These knishes are filling and make a great lunch away from home or snack.

2 pounds potatoes, peeled and chopped
2 cups water
1 small onion, peeled and finely chopped
1/2 pound mushrooms, finely chopped
1 teaspoon oil
1/4 teaspoon salt
Dash of pepper
1/2 cup kasha (roasted buckwheat)
1-1/2 cups vegetable broth or water (recipe on
   page 70)
1/2 teaspoon turmeric
1/4 teaspoon salt
1-1/2 cups unbleached white flour
1-1/4 teaspoons baking powder

Cook potatoes in boiling water in a covered pot for 20 minutes. Drain.

Sauté onion and mushrooms with oil and 1/4 teaspoon salt and dash of pepper in a frying pan over medium heat for 3 minutes. Add kasha and continue cooking for 1 minute longer. Finally, add vegetable broth or water. Simmer 10 minutes, stirring occasionally.

Mash cooked potatoes and divide into thirds. Stir 1/3 of the mashed potatoes into the sautéed onion/mushroom/kasha mixture. Mix remaining mashed potatoes with turmeric, salt, flour, and baking powder to create a dough. Knead dough for a few minutes. Then, roll dough out on floured surface until 1/4-inch thick. Cut dough into 4" x 4" squares (about 8). Place 1/8th of potato/onion/kasha mixture on each square. Fold corners of dough in and pinch dough tight in center.

Preheat oven to 375 degrees. Place knishes (pinched side down) on lightly oiled cookie sheet. Bake at 375 degrees for 45 minutes. Serve warm.

Total calories per serving: 455
Fat: 3%   Total Fat as % of Daily Value: 5%   Protein: 12 grams   Iron: 4 mg
Carbohydrates: 98 grams   Calcium: 43 mg   Dietary fiber: 8.8 grams

MUSHROOM BARLEY KUGEL

(Serves 8)

This kugel recipe contains no eggs. You can also substitute brown rice for the barley.

1 cup barley
4 cups water
1/2 pound mushrooms
1 small onion, peeled and finely chopped
2 teaspoons oil
1/4 cup unbleached white flour
1 cup vegetable broth (recipe on page 70)
1 cup lite (lowfat) soy milk
Salt and pepper to taste

Preheat oven to 375 degrees. Cook barley in water in a large pot for 1 hour and 15 minutes.

Meanwhile, sauté mushrooms and onion with oil in a frying pan over medium heat for 3 minutes. Dissolve flour in soy milk and broth and then add to sautéed mushrooms and onions. Simmer 5 minutes longer, stirring constantly. Add salt and pepper to taste. Add cooked barley to mixture and mix well.

Press barley/mushroom mixture into a lightly oiled 9" x 9" x 2" baking pan. Bake at 375 degrees for 30 minutes. Serve warm.

Total calories per serving: 140
Fat: 2 grams   Total Fat as % of Daily Value:3%   Protein: 5 grams   Iron: 1.3 mg
Carbohydrates: 27 grams   Calcium:15 mg   Dietary fiber: 2.5 grams

MUSHROOM/ NOODLE KUGEL

(Serves 8)

This kugel recipe contains no eggs and is absolutely delicious. Experiment with different varieties of mushrooms.

12-ounce package eggless noodles
10 cups water
3/4 pound mushrooms, finely chopped
1 onion, finely chopped
2 teaspoons oil
Salt and pepper to taste
1 cup soy milk
2 Tablespoons cornstarch

Cook noodles in boiling water in a large pot for 8 minutes until tender. Drain.

Meanwhile, preheat oven to 350 degrees. Sauté mushrooms and onion with oil in a frying pan for 3 minutes. Add seasonings. Dissolve cornstarch in soy milk and add to sautéed mushrooms and onions. Simmer 2 minutes longer, stirring constantly.

In a lightly oiled baking pan, put a layer of 1/3 noodles followed by 1/3 mushroom/onion mixture. Repeat process two more times. Bake at 350 degrees for 45 minutes. Serve warm.

Total calories per serving: 168
Fat: 3 grams   Total Fat as % of Daily Value: 5%   Protein: 6 grams   Iron: 1.7 mg
Carbohydrates: 31 grams   Calcium:24 mg   Dietary fiber: 2.1 grams

NORTH AFRICAN PEA DISH
(Serves 5)

This simple North African dish combines leek (a type of onion) with peas.

1 leek
1 small onion, peeled and finely chopped
2 cups fresh or frozen peas
1 teaspoon oil
1/4 cup water

Rinse leek well and chop off bottom roots. Finely chop entire leek(including leaves). Sauté leek and remaining ingredients in a small frying pan over medium heat for 5 minutes. Serve warm.

Total calories per serving: 68
Fat: 1 gram   Total Fat as % of Daily Value: 2%   Protein: 4 grams   Iron: 1.2 mg
Carbohydrates: 11 grams   Calcium: 24 mg   Dietary fiber: 4.7 grams

POLISH SWEET AND SOUR CABBAGE
(Serves 8)

People rarely seem to use caraway seeds, except when bread baking. This recipe adds apples, raisins, and caraway seeds to cabbage and can be prepared quickly. Traditionally, sugar would be used instead of the corn or rice syrup.

1 head cabbage (about 3 pounds; purple or green)
1 onion, peeled and finely chopped
2 apples, cored and chopped
1/2 cup water
1 cup raisins
2 teaspoons caraway seeds
2 Tablespoons corn or rice syrup
1/4 cup apple cider vinegar

Remove core from cabbage and chop cabbage into bite-size pieces. Sauté cabbage, onion, and apples in water in a large pot over medium heat for 10 minutes. Add remaining ingredients and simmer 3 minutes longer. Serve warm.

Total calories per serving: 143
Fat: <1 gram Total Fat as % of Daily Value: <1%   Protein: 3 grams   Iron: 1.7 mg
Carbohydrates: 36 grams   Calcium: 98 mg   Dietary fiber: 8.3 grams

POTATO KNISHES
(Serves 6 -- 2 each)

Knishes are popular in many cities throughout the United States. Often the dough contains eggs. This recipe is eggless.

**3 pounds potatoes, peeled and chopped
3 cups water
2 onions, peeled and finely chopped
2 teaspoons oil
1/2 teaspoon salt
1/4 teaspoon pepper
1 teaspoon turmeric
1/2 teaspoon salt
3 cups unbleached white flour
2 teaspoons baking powder**

Cook potatoes in boiling water in a covered pot for 20 minutes. Drain.

Sauté onions with oil and 1/2 teaspoon salt and dash of pepper in a frying pan over medium heat until onions are soft.

Mash cooked potatoes and divide mixture in half. Stir half the mashed potatoes with sautéed onion mixture. Mix remaining mashed potatoes with turmeric, salt, flour, and baking powder to create a dough. Knead dough for a few minutes. Then, roll dough out on floured surface until 1/4-inch thick. Cut dough into 4" x 4" squares (about 12). Place 1/12th of potato/onion mixture on each square. Fold corners of dough in and pinch dough tight in center.

Preheat oven to 375 degrees. Place knishes (pinched side down) on lightly oiled cookie sheet. Bake at 375 degrees for 45 minutes. Serve warm with mustard or sauerkraut.

Total calories per serving: 429
Fat: 2 grams Total Fat as % of Daily Value:3% Protein:10 grams Iron: 3.4 mg
Carbohydrates: 92 grams Calcium: 36 mg Dietary fiber: 6.3 grams

POTATO KUGEL
(Serves 8)

Try this wonderful eggless potato pudding containing cauliflower.

6 potatoes, peeled and grated
2 onions, peeled and grated
10-ounce package frozen cauliflower, cooked and
**   mashed**
1/2 cup unbleached white flour
1/2 teaspoon baking powder
1 teaspoon salt
Dash of pepper

Preheat oven to 350 degrees.
    Mix all the ingredients together in a large bowl. Pour into a lightly oiled baking pan and bake at 350 degrees for one hour until brown. Serve warm.

Total calories per serving: 145
Fat:4 grams   Total Fat as % of Daily Value:<1%   Protein:4 grams   Iron: 0.9 mg
Carbohydrates: 33 grams   Calcium:16 mg   Dietary fiber: 3.6 grams

POTATO LATKES
(Serves 4)

Potato latkes are pancakes traditionally served during Chanukah. This recipe contains no eggs and is delicious topped with applesauce or other cooked fruit.

1-1/2 pounds potatoes, peeled and grated
1 medium onion, peeled and grated
3 Tablespoons cornstarch
1 Tablespoon fresh parsley, finely chopped
Dash of pepper
2 Tablespoons tamari or soy sauce

Mix all the ingredients together in a large bowl. Form 3-inch patties and fry in lightly oiled pan over medium heat for 10 minutes. Flip latkes and fry for another 10 minutes until crisp on both sides. Serve warm.

Total calories per serving: 216
Fat: 4 grams   Total Fat as % of Daily Value: 6%   Protein: 4 grams   Iron: 0.9 mg
Carbohydrates: 43 grams   Calcium: 25 mg   Dietary fiber: 3.9 grams

ROMANIAN
SWEET PASTA
(Serves 8)

A friend from Romania taught me a recipe similar to this one.
Traditionally, honey and more nuts are used.

1 pound eggless pasta
12 cups water
1 cup maple syrup
1/2 cup walnuts, ground or 1/3 cup poppy seeds,
    ground
1/2 teaspoon lemon rind, minced
1-1/2 cups raisins
1/2 teaspoon powdered cloves
1 teaspoon cinnamon

Cook pasta in boiling water until done. Drain.

Heat maple syrup and walnuts or poppy seeds in a large pot over medium heat for 2 minutes. Add lemon rind, raisins, clove powder, and cinnamon. Continue cooking for 3 more minutes. Add cooked pasta. Mix well and serve warm. You can also pour the mixture into a baking dish and bake at 350 degrees for 20 minutes before serving.

Total calories per serving: 395
Fat:5 grams   Total Fat as % of Daily Value:8%   Protein:8 grams   Iron: 2.1 mg
Carbohydrates: 83 grams   Calcium:37 mg   Dietary fiber: 3.6 grams

RUSSIAN BAKED PEPPERS
(Serves 6)

I first saw this dish in delis in the Russian section of Brighton Beach, New York. Traditionally, more oil is used.

4 green, yellow, and/or red bell peppers
3 Tablespoons red wine vinegar
1 teaspoon olive oil
1 teaspoon garlic powder
1/4 teaspoon salt

Preheat oven to 400 degrees.

Cut peppers in half length-wise. Remove and discard seeds. Cut peppers into thin strips. Place on a cookie sheet. Sprinkle peppers with vinegar and oil. Then sprinkle with garlic powder and salt. Bake peppers at 400 degrees for 20 minutes. Serve warm.

Total calories per serving: 21
Fat: 1 gram   Total Fat as % of Daily Value: 2%   Protein: <1 gram   Iron: 0.6 mg
Carbohydrates: 3 grams   Calcium:3 mg   Dietary fiber: 0.7 grams

RUSSIAN COOKED CUCUMBERS
(Serves 5)

Here's a simple, yet creative way, to use cucumbers. This quick and easy method of cooking cucumbers uses fresh dill.

2 medium cucumbers, peeled and thinly sliced
2 teaspoons margarine
1 small onion, peeled and minced
1 Tablespoon fresh dill, finely chopped
Salt and pepper to taste

Sauté all the ingredients in a large frying pan over medium heat for 5 minutes. Serve warm.

Total calories per serving: 31
Fat: 2 grams   Total Fat as % of Daily Value: 3%   Protein: 1 gram   Iron: 0.3 mg
Carbohydrates: 4 grams   Calcium: 18 mg   Dietary fiber: 1.7 grams

RUSSIAN POTATOES WITH CHERRY SAUCE

(Serves 4)

Traditionally, this dish is made with sour cherries and sugar is added. I've used sweet cherries instead and eliminated the added sugar.

1 pound potatoes, peeled and chopped
4 cups water
1 Tablespoon whole wheat pastry flour
1-1/2 teaspoons oil
2 Tablespoons water
1 pound sweet cherries, pitted
Salt to taste

Cook potatoes in boiling water in a covered pot for 20 minutes. Drain.

Meanwhile, in a separate frying pan, heat the flour in oil to form a roux. Add the water and cherries. Cook over medium heat for 5 minutes, stirring occasionally.

Serve warm cherry sauce over cooked potatoes.

Total calories per serving: 201
Fat: 3 grams   Total Fat as % of Daily Value: 5%   Protein: 4 grams   Iron: 0.9 mg
Carbohydrates: 43 grams   Calcium: 27 mg   Dietary fiber: 3.8 grams

RUSSIAN RED LOBIO
(Serves 6)

Traditionally, this Russian bean dish contains a lot more oil and nuts, and thus is much higher in fat. This version is just as delicious.

3 cups cooked red kidney beans, drained (two 15-1/2 ounce cans)
4 scallions, chopped
1/4 cup red wine vinegar
2 teaspoons olive oil
2 Tablespoons fresh parsley, finely chopped
1/4 cup walnuts, chopped or whole

Mix all the ingredients together in a large bowl. Cover bowl and refrigerate for at least one hour (preferably overnight) before serving chilled.

Total calories per serving: 159
Fat:5 grams   Total Fat as % of Daily Value:8%   Protein:8 grams   Iron: 2.1 mg
Carbohydrates: 22 grams   Calcium: 43 mg   Dietary fiber: 10.7 grams

SAUERKRAUT KNISHES
(Serves 4 -- 2 each)

These delicious knishes should be eaten right after they are baked so that they do not become soggy.

2 pounds potatoes, peeled and chopped
2 cups water
1-1/2 cups sauerkraut
1/4 teaspoon caraway seeds
1/8 cup water
1/2 teaspoon turmeric
1/4 teaspoon salt
1-1/2 cups unbleached white flour
1-1/4 teaspoons baking powder

Cook potatoes in 2 cups boiling water in a covered pot for 20 minutes. Drain.

Heat sauerkraut and caraway seeds in 1/8 cup water in a small pot over medium heat for 5 minutes.

Mash cooked potatoes and divide mixture into thirds. Stir 1/3 mashed potatoes with sauerkraut mixture. Mix remaining mashed potatoes with turmeric, salt, flour, and baking powder to create a dough. Knead dough for a few minutes. Then roll dough out on floured surface until 1/4-inch thick. Cut dough into 4" x 4" squares (about 8). Place 1/8th of sauerkraut mixture on each square. Fold corners of dough in and pinch dough tight in center.

Preheat oven to 375 degrees. Place knishes (pinched side down) on lightly oiled cookie sheet. Bake at 375 degrees for 45 minutes. Serve warm.

Total calories per serving: 369
Fat: 1 gram   Total Fat as % of Daily Value: 2%   Protein: 9 grams   Iron: 3.9 mg
Carbohydrates: 82 grams   Calcium: 51 mg   Dietary fiber: 7.7 grams

SPINACH KNISHES

(Serves 4 -- 2 each)

These knishes are perfect to take to the office. Simply heat them up in an oven or microwave and you'll have a delicious hot lunch.

2 pounds potatoes, peeled and chopped
2 cups water
1 small onion, peeled and finely chopped
2 teaspoons oil
1/4 teaspoon salt
Dash of pepper
1-1/2 cups cooked spinach (fresh or frozen)
1/2 teaspoon turmeric
1/4 teaspoon salt
1-1/2 cups unbleached white flour
1-1/4 teaspoons baking powder

Cook potatoes in boiling water in a covered pot for 20 minutes. Drain.

Sauté onions with oil and 1/4 teaspoon salt and pepper in a frying pan over medium heat for 2 minutes. Add cooked spinach and continue cooking for 2 minutes longer.

Mash cooked potatoes and divide mixture into thirds. Stir 1/3 mashed potatoes with sautéed onion/spinach mixture. Mix remaining mashed potatoes with turmeric, salt, flour, and baking powder to create a dough. Knead dough for a few minutes. Then roll dough out on floured surface until 1/4-inch thick. Cut dough into 4" x 4" squares (about 8). Place 1/8th of potato/onion/spinach mixture on each square. Fold corners of dough in and pinch dough tight in center.

Preheat oven to 375 degrees. Place knishes (pinched side down) on lightly oiled cookie sheet. Bake at 375 degrees for 45 minutes. Serve warm.

Total calories per serving: 398
Fat: 3 grams   Total Fat as % of Daily Value: 5%   Protein:11 grams   Iron: 3.8 mg
Carbohydrates: 83 grams   Calcium: 134 mg   Dietary fiber: 7.9 grams

SYRIAN-STYLE OKRA WITH DRIED FRUIT

(Serves 4)

This unique dish combines different types of juice with dried fruit, chopped lemon, and okra. Your guests will absolutely enjoy it.

1/2 pound okra, chopped
1/2 small onion, peeled and finely chopped
1 teaspoon oil
1 Tablespoon water
1-1/2 cups dried fruit (about 8 ounces prunes, apricots, raisins, etc.)
1/2 cup prune juice
1/2 cup tomato juice
1/4 lemon, minced (rind and fruit)

Stir-fry okra and onion with oil and water in a large frying pan for 5 minutes over medium heat. Add dried fruit, juices, and lemon. Simmer 15 minutes, stirring often. Serve warm or chilled.

Total calories per serving: 267
Fat: 1 gram   Total Fat as % of Daily Value: 2%   Protein: 3 grams   Iron: 3.4 mg
Carbohydrates: 68 grams   Calcium: 54 mg   Dietary fiber: 8.5 grams

TURKISH PILAF
(Serves 6)

This Turkish pilaf consists of brown rice, dried fruit, chopped nuts, and a touch of cinnamon. Try different types of dried fruit and nuts.

1-1/2 cups brown rice
4 cups water
1/4 cup dried prunes, chopped
1/4 cup dried apricots, chopped
2 Tablespoons slivered almonds
2 Tablespoons shelled pistachio nuts
1 teaspoon cinnamon

Cook the brown rice in boiling water in a covered pot for 45 mintues. Stir in remaining ingredients and serve warm.

Total calories per serving: 203
Fat: 4 grams   Total Fat as % of Daily Value: 6%   Protein: 4 grams   Iron: 1.3 mg
Carbohydrates: 39 grams   Calcium: 20 mg   Dietary fiber: 2.8 grams

YEMENITE GRAPE/ PINE NUT STUFFING
(Serves 12)

This unique stuffing combines different types of dried fruit with pine nuts, olives, and grapes. It is an absolutely delicious dish.

1-1/2 pounds seedless grapes
1 cup pine nuts
1/2 cup black olives, pitted
1/2 cup dried figs, chopped
1/2 cup dried dates, chopped
2 teaspoons coriander
Salt and pepper to taste

Place all the ingredients in a food processor bowl. Blend together for 1-2 minutes. Serve stuffing at room temperature or chilled, garnished with a few whole grapes.

Total calories per serving: 136
Fat:6 grams   Total Fat as % of Daily Value:9%   Protein:3.4 grams   Iron:1.5 mg
Carbohydrates: 21 grams   Calcium: 25 mg   Dietary fiber: 1.9 grams

DESSERTS

ALMOND COOKIES
(Makes 2 dozen)

Bananas are used as a binder in this recipe to replace eggs. Children and adults will enjoy these cookies.

2 cups almonds
1/2 cup maple syrup
3 ripe bananas, peeled and mashed
1 cup whole wheat pastry flour
1-1/2 cups unbleached white flour

Preheat oven to 350 degrees.

Meanwhile, grind 1-3/4 cups almonds into a meal in a food processor (reserving 1/4 cup whole almonds). In a separate large bowl, cream together the maple syrup and mashed bananas. Add almond meal and flours. Mix well.

Divide and roll dough into 24 balls. Press one whole almond on top of each ball. Bake on lightly oiled cookie sheet at 350 degrees for 12 minutes. Cool and serve.

Total calories per cookie: 137
Fat: 6 grams   Total Fat as % of Daily Value: 9%   Protein: 4 grams   Iron: 0.9 mg
Carbohydrates: 19 grams   Calcium: 34 mg   Dietary fiber: 1.8 grams

APPLE SPICE CAKE
(Serves 9)

This recipe is especially fun to make in the fall when many different varieties of apples are available in stores.

3 cups whole wheat pastry flour
5 teaspoons margarine
2 teaspoons baking powder
1 teaspoon baking soda
1 teaspoon cinnamon
1 teaspoon nutmeg
1/2 teaspoon allspice
1/4 teaspoon ground cloves
1-1/2 cups water
1/2 cup maple syrup
2 teaspoons vanilla
3 apples, cored, quartered, and sliced
Raisins or other dried fruit, chopped

Preheat oven to 350 degrees.

Mix all the ingredients together in a large bowl, except apples and raisins. Pour half the batter into a lightly oiled 9" x 12" pan. Lay apple slices on top of batter and cover with remaining batter. Decorate with raisins or dried fruit. Bake at 350 degrees for 30 minutes. Cool before removing from pan.

Total calories per serving: 251
Fat: 3 grams   Total Fat as % of Daily Value: 5%   Protein: 6 grams   Iron: 1.6 mg
Carbohydrates: 54 grams   Calcium: 28 mg   Dietary fiber: 6.9 grams

APPLE TURNOVERS

(Serves 8)

These delicious turnovers contain no added sugar. I use apple cider as the sweetener. You can substitute other chopped fruit such as pears and peaches for the apples.

1-1/2 pounds apples, cored and finely chopped
1/2 cup raisins
1/2 teaspoon cinnamon
1/4 cup apple cider
8 sheets phyllo dough
1 teaspoon margarine

Cook apples, raisins, cinnamon, and cider in a small covered pot over medium-low heat for 15 minutes. Stir occasionally. Remove pot from stove and allow to cool for 5 minutes. Drain excess liquid from mixture.

Preheat oven to 375 degrees. Melt margarine in a small pan. Take 8 sheets of phyllo dough stacked one on top of another and cut it into 8 squares. Place 3 heaping Tablespoons of apple/raisin filling on each square. Fold ends of phyllo dough in and place each turnover, with folded ends down, onto a lightly oiled cookie sheet. Brush each turnover with a little melted margarine. Bake 30 minutes at 375 degrees until light brown on top. Serve warm.

Total calories per serving: 147
Fat: 1 gram   Total Fat as % of Daily Value: 2%   Protein: 3 grams   Iron: 1.2 mg
Carbohydrates: 35 grams   Calcium: 27 mg   Dietary fiber: 3 grams

BAKED FRUIT
(Serves 8)

Baked fruit is especially popular among Polish Jews. You can substitute nectarines or sweet plums for the peaches, and apples for the pears. Experiment with other varieties of dried fruit, too.

3 pounds ripe peaches, pits removed and thinly sliced
2 pounds ripe pears, cored and thinly sliced
1/2 pound fresh or dried figs, chopped
1 teaspoon cinnamon
1 cup apple juice

Preheat oven to 375 degrees.
   Mix the fruit and cinnamon together and pour fruit into a 2-quart baking dish. Pour juice into dish and bake covered for 45 minutes at 375 degrees. Serve warm.

Total calories per serving: 217
Fat: 1 gram   Total Fat as % of Daily Value: 2 %   Protein: 2 grams   Iron: 1.2 mg
Carbohydrates: 56 grams   Calcium: 60 mg   Dietary fiber: 8.7 grams

FRUIT COMPOTE
(Serves 10)

Dried fruit can be purchased in marketplaces throughout the world. This is a popular Russian dish. The compote tastes like pudding once it has simmered for an hour. Experiment with different varieties of dried fruit.

2 cups dried peaches, cut in half
2 cups whole pitted dried prunes
2 cups dried apricots
1 cup raisins
1 stick cinnamon, broken in half
4 whole cloves
4 cups apple cider

Mix all the ingredients together in a large pot. Simmer covered over a medium heat for 1 hour. Serve warm.

Total calories per serving: 375
Fat: 1 gram   Total Fat as % of Daily Value: 2%   Protein: 4 grams   Iron: 5 mg
Carbohydrates: 98 grams   Calcium: 62 mg   Dietary fiber: 11.8 grams

GREEK ZUCCHINI PASTRIES
(Serves 8)

This recipe is a little bit complicated to prepare; however, it is a great dessert to serve at a party and worth the effort.

1-1/2 pounds zucchini, grated
2 Tablespoons water
2 teaspoons cornstarch
2 Tablespoons chopped walnuts
1 teaspoon cinnamon
1/4 cup maple syrup
2 teaspoons margarine
8 sheets phyllo dough

Sauté zucchini with water and cornstarch in a large frying pan over medium heat for 5 minutes. Add walnuts, cinnamon, and maple syrup. Continue cooking for 5 minutes longer, stirring often.

Melt margarine in a separate small pan over low heat. Preheat oven to 375 degrees. Take phyllo dough and separate into two piles of four sheets. Cut each pile into four equal size squares, for a total of eight squares. Place 1/8th of mixture in the middle of each square. Fold ends of phyllo dough under. Brush phyllo dough with melted margarine. Place on lightly oiled cookie sheet with folded ends down. Bake at 375 degrees for 20 minutes until light brown. Allow to cool for a few minutes before removing from pan. Serve warm.

Total calories per serving: 122
Fat: 2 grams   Total Fat as % of Daily Value: 3%   Protein: 4 grams   Iron: 1.2 mg
Carbohydrates: 24 grams   Calcium: 35 mg   Dietary fiber: 1.5 grams

HAMENTASHEN
(Serves 15)

Here's an eggless version of hamentashen, the popular baked treat served during Purim. If you are unable to purchase prune or poppy seed filling in your local supermarket, simply puree a few prunes with a little fruit juice.

1-1/2 cups unbleached white flour
1-1/2 cups whole wheat pastry flour
1-1/2 teaspoons baking powder
1/3 cup canola oil
2/3 cup water
1/2 cup applesauce
3 Tablespoons orange juice
5 Tablespoons prune or poppy seed filling

Preheat oven to 350 degrees.

Mix all the ingredients, except filling, together in a large bowl. Knead dough for a few minutes. Separate into 3 balls. Cover balls with a slightly damp towel and refrigerate dough for about 3 hours. Remove from refrigerator and roll balls of dough out to 1/8-inch thickness. Cut out approximately 15 four-inch rounds. Place 1 teaspoon prune or poppy seed filling in center. (Filling can be bought in supermarkets and some natural food stores). Form a triangle out of the dough by folding in edges, but still leaving some space in the middle of the dough for the filling to remain mostly uncovered.

Bake at 350 degrees for 30 minutes until dough is brown. Serve.

Total calories per pastry: 141
Fat: 5 grams   Total Fat as % of Daily Value: 8%   Protein: 3 grams   Iron: 1 mg
Carbohydrates: 22 grams   Calcium: 8 mg   Dietary fiber: 2 grams

MOROCCAN COUSCOUS
(Serves 4)

Here's a quick dessert that is absolutely delicious. Try substituting different types of nuts or dried fruit.

1 cup orange juice or other juice
1/2 cup water
1 cup couscous
1/2 cup water
1/4 cup pitted dates, finely chopped
1/4 cup raisins
1/4 cup slivered almonds
1 teaspoon cinnamon
1/2 cup water

Bring juice and 1/2 cup water to a boil in a small pot. Remove from heat. Stir in couscous and allow to sit covered for 5 minutes.

Meanwhile, in a separate pan, sauté dates, raisins, almonds, and cinnamon in 1/2 cup water for 2 minutes. Add cooked couscous. Mix well and serve warm.

Total calories per serving: 253
Fat: 4 grams   Total Fat as % of Daily Value: 6%   Protein:6 grams   Iron: 1.1 mg
Carbohydrates: 48 grams   Calcium: 44 mg   Dietary fiber: 2.3 grams

NORTH AFRICAN BARLEY PUDDING
(Serves 5)

Many Americans have eaten rice pudding at some point in their lives. This pudding substitutes barley for rice and is sweetened with maple syrup. Traditionally sugar is used for the sweetener in North Africa. You can experiment with different types of nuts or substitute dried fruit for the nuts. Children will love this dessert!

1 cup barley, uncooked
3-1/2 cups water
1 Tablespoon pine nuts
1 Tablespoon slivered almonds
1 Tablespoon pistachios
1 cup maple syrup

Cook barley in water in a large pot over medium heat for 1-1/2 hours, until very soft. Stir in remaining ingredients and continue heating for 2 minutes, stirring constantly. Serve warm or chilled.

Total calories per serving: 330
Fat: 3 grams   Total Fat as % of Daily Value: 5%   Protein: 5 grams   Iron: 1.2 mg
Carbohydrates: 72 grams   Calcium: 25 mg   Dietary fiber: 2.9 grams

RICE PUDDING
(Serves 6)

Instead of using cow's milk in this popular dessert, I've substituted water or soy milk and added bananas to create a creamy texture.

1 cup brown rice
2 cups water
2/3 cup raisins
2 ripe bananas, peeled and chopped
1/2 cup water or soy milk
1 teaspoon cinnamon
1 teaspoon vanilla extract
1/4 teaspoon nutmeg

Cook rice, water, and raisins together in a large covered pot over medium heat until rice is done (about 1 hour).

Preheat oven to 350 degrees. Meanwhile, place cooked rice mixture in a food processor or blender cup. Add remaining ingredients and blend until creamy. Pour mixture into a small glass loaf pan. Bake at 350 degrees for 20 minutes. Serve warm or cold as leftovers.

Total calories per serving: 190
Fat: 1 gram   Total Fat as % of Daily Value: 2%   Protein: 3 grams   Iron: 1 mg
Carbohydrates: 45 grams   Calcium: 16 mg   Dietary fiber: 3.1 grams

ROMANIAN APRICOT DUMPLINGS

(Serves 8 -- 3 dumplings each)

Although this dessert is not easy to prepare, it's so good that it's worth the effort. You can substitute different fruit such as peaches.

4 pounds potatoes, peeled and chopped
10 cups water
1/2 teaspoon salt
1/2 cup maple syrup
2 cups whole wheat pastry flour
6 ripe apricots, pitted
1 teaspoon oil
2 teaspoons cinnamon

Cook potatoes in salted water in large pot over medium heat until tender. Drain and cool, saving liquid to use later. Mash potatoes once (not too much). Stir in maple syrup. Slowly add flour to make a dough that's not too thick, but not sticky either.

Chop apricots into quarters. Take a handful of dough and flatten with your palm. Put chopped apricot quarter in center of dough. Roll dough into a ball, covering apricot. Repeat process to make approximately 24 dumplings.

Bring potato water that was set aside earlier back to a boil. Add oil. Place 6 dumplings into boiling water. Dumplings are done when they float to the top of the pot. Remove from boiling water and strain them in a colander. Repeat this process four times. Sprinkle dumplings with cinnamon and serve warm.

Total calories per serving: 363
Fat: 1 gram   Total Fat as % of Daily Value: 2%   Protein: 8 grams   Iron: 1.8 mg
Carbohydrates: 82 grams   Calcium: 37 mg   Dietary fiber: 8.8 grams

ROMANIAN WHEAT BERRY PUDDING
(Serves 8)

Wheat berries are a very inexpensive grain sold in health food stores. Few people know how to creatively prepare this grain. This Romanian pudding is exquisite.

2 cups wheat berries
7 cups water
1/2 cup walnuts
1-1/2 cups raisins
1 cup maple syrup
1 teaspoon cinnamon
1/2 teaspoon clove powder

Soak wheat berries in water overnight in a large pot for about 8-10 hours.

Bring water and wheat berries to a boil. Then simmer in covered pot for 3 hours until wheat berries are tender. Add more water if needed. Strain and rinse cooked wheat berries two or three times to get rid of excess starch.

Take 1/4 of the cooked wheat berries and place in a food processor bowl. Grind in food processor for a few minutes. Pour ground wheat berries into a large bowl. Add walnuts, raisins, maple syrup, cinnamon, and clove powder. Stir in remaining whole cooked wheat berries. Mix well and serve warm, or chill and slice.

Total calories per serving: 402
Fat: 6 grams Total Fat as % of Daily Value:9%   Protein:9 grams   Iron: 2.3 mg
Carbohydrates: 84 grams   Calcium: 45 mg   Dietary fiber: 7.7 grams

RUSSIAN FRUIT PUDDING
(Serves 5)

*This Russian pudding is absolutely delicious. Experiment with
different varieties of fruit such as peaches, nectarines, etc.*

**3 apples, peeled and chopped
3 pears, peeled and chopped
2 plums, peeled and chopped
2 cups water
1 teaspoon cinnamon
3 Tablespoons cornstarch or potato starch for Passover
1/2 cup water**

Place chopped fruit, 2 cups water, and cinnamon in a small covered pot. Simmer over
medium heat for 20 minutes until fruit is well cooked. Puree mixture in a blender
and return to the pot. Dissolve cornstarch in 1/2 cup water and add to cooked fruit
mixture. Continue simmering for 2 minutes longer. The pudding will thicken.

Pour into 5 small bowls and chill at least 2 hours before serving.

Total calories per serving: 134
Fat: 1 gram   Total Fat as % of Daily Value:1%   Protein: 1 gram   Iron: 0.3 mg
Carbohydrates: 34 grams   Calcium: 15 mg   Dietary fiber: 4.5 grams

SWEET FRUIT KUGEL
(Serves 8)

Mashed bananas are used as a binder instead of eggs in this sweet kugel (noodle pudding). Try using different varieties of fruit such as peaches or nectarines. Experiment with other types of dried fruit.

12-ounce package eggless noodles
4 quarts water
3 ripe bananas, peeled and mashed
1 teaspoon cinnamon
2 apples, cored and chopped
2 pears, cored and chopped
1/2 cup raisins

Bring water to a boil, add noodles, and lower heat. Simmer for 10 minutes until noodles are tender. Drain.

Preheat oven to 350 degrees. Mix cooked noodles with mashed bananas and cinnamon. Place 1/3 noodle mixture in a lightly oiled 9" x 9" x2" square pan. Place 1/3 chopped fruit and raisins on top of noodle mixture. Repeat process two more times. Bake at 350 degrees for 45 minutes. Serve warm.

Total calories per serving: 231
Fat: 1 gram   Total Fat as % of Daily Value: 2%   Protein: 5 grams   Iron: 1.5 mg
Carbohydrates: 54 grams   Calcium: 23 mg   Dietary fiber: 4.5 grams

SYRIAN WHEAT PUDDING
(Serves 8)

This unique Syrian pudding traditionally would contain more nuts, and thus more fat. This version is lower in fat and absolutely delicious.

1-1/2 cups bulgur (cracked wheat)
4 cups water
1 cup raisins
1/2 teaspoon caraway seeds
1 Tablespoon shelled pistachio nuts
1 Tablespoon shelled walnuts, chopped
1/4 cup maple syrup

Place bulgur, water, raisins, and caraway seeds in a covered pot. Cook over medium heat for 30 minutes. Stir occasionally. Add nuts and syrup. Simmer 5 minutes longer. Serve warm. Cold leftovers are good, too.

Total calories per serving: 206
Fat: 2 grams Total Fat as % of Daily Value: 2%   Protein: 5 grams   Iron: 1.3 mg
Carbohydrates: 45 grams   Calcium: 26 mg   Dietary fiber: 4.4 grams

BEVERAGES

ALMOND MILK
(Serves 12)

Almond milk is traditionally drunk in small portions by Iraqi Jews to break fast after Yom Kippur. It is a delicious alternative to cow's milk. You can also pour a small amount of almond milk over rice pudding (recipe on page 180) before serving.

3/4 cup raw almonds
2-1/4 cups boiling water

Place almonds and boiling water in a blender cup. Blend at high speed for 3 minutes. Strain liquid through cheesecloth or muslin. Chill milk and serve.

Total calories per serving: 48
Fat: 4 grams Total Fat as % of Daily Value: 6% Protein: 2 grams Iron: 0.3 mg
Carbohydrates: 2 grams Calcium: 22 mg Dietary fiber: not available

CELERY SODA
(Serves 5)

Celery Soda is traditionally found in Jewish-American restaurants. Here I've substituted apple juice concentrate for artificial sweeteners.

9 stalks celery, chopped
1/3 cup water
4 Tablespoons apple juice concentrate
1 liter seltzer water, chilled

Put celery through a juicer and add water and apple juice concentrate to liquid. If you do not own a juicer, liquefy the celery (one handful at a time) with water and apple juice concentrate in a blender cup at high speed. Strain celery liquid through muslin or cheesecloth and save liquid.

Add celery liquid (about 2 cups) to seltzer water and serve chilled.

Total calories per serving: 34
Fat: <1 gram Total Fat as % of Daily Value: <1% Protein: 1 gram Iron: 0.5 mg
Carbohydrates: 8 grams Calcium: 39 mg Dietary fiber: not available

"EGG" CREAM SODA
(Serves 4)

When I was a very young child, my grandparents owned a candy store in Brooklyn, New York. Egg cream sodas were always very popular. Traditionally, they are made with cow's milk. Here I use soy milk. Try using different flavors of soy milks and syrups for variety.

**3 cups soy milk, chilled
3/4 cup seltzer water
4 Tablespoons non-dairy chocolate syrup**

Pour soy milk into four tall glasses. Slowly add seltzer water and chocolate syrup. Stir with a spoon for a few seconds. Serve immediately.

Total calories per serving: 165
Fat: 6 grams Total Fat as % of Daily Value: 9%   Protein: 8 grams   Iron: 1.4 mg
Carbohydrates: 23 grams   Calcium: 69 mg   Dietary fiber: 0.5 grams

LEMONADE
(Serves 6)

Greek Jews traditionally drink lemonade to break their fast after Yom Kippur. Lemonade is also very popular in the Middle East. Usually a lot of sugar is added to the lemonade to make it sweet. Instead, I add sliced oranges to sweeten the lemonade slightly.

4 lemons, juiced, seeds removed
8 cups water
2 oranges, sliced, seeds removed

Place all the ingredients in a large glass jar. Refrigerate at least 3 hours before serving. Serve chilled.

Total calories per serving: 26
Fat: <1 gram   Total Fat as % of Daily Value: <1% Protein: <1 gram   Iron: 0.1 mg
Carbohydrates: 7 grams   Calcium: 20 mg   Dietary fiber: 1.3 grams

MINT TEA
(Serves 6)

Anyone who has ever grown mint in his or her garden knows how prolific it is. Mint tea is quite simple to prepare and very refreshing. Experiment with different varieties of mint.

4 cups fresh mint leaves, chopped, stems removed
10 cups boiling water

Place all the ingredients in a large pot and allow to cool. Once cool, pour into a large pitcher and refrigerate for at least 3 hours. The longer it sits before serving, the stronger the tea will be. Strain tea leaves and serve chilled.

Total calories per serving: 14
Fat: 0 grams   Total Fat as % of Daily Value: 0%   Protein: 1 gra,   Iron: n/a
Carbohydrates: 2 grams   Calcium: n/a   Dietary fiber: n/a

PASSOVER DISHES

BREAKFASTS
Blueberry/Banana Matzo Meal Pancakes (pg. 32)

SPREADS
Eggplant Caviar (pg. 43)
Eggplant Spread (pg. 44)

SALADS
Beet Salad (pg. 73)
Israeli Carrot Salad (pg. 75)
Moroccan Beet Greens Salad (pg. 79)
Pineapple/Avocado/Tangerine Salad (pg. 80)
Russian Charoset (pg. 83)
Russian Potato and Beet Salad (pg. 85)
Turkish Mandarin Salad (pg. 87)

MAIN DISHES
Eggplant Stew over Baked Potatoes (pg. 96)
Passover Vegetarian Kishke (pg. 106)
Russian Potato and Mushroom Croquettes (pg. 116)

SIDE DISHES

Baked Carrots (pg. 138)
Broccoli and Lemon Sauce (pg. 140)
Cabbage Sauté (pg. 142)
Carrot and Cabbage Sauté (pg. 143)
Italian Sautéed Chicory (pg. 149)
Russian Baked Peppers (pg. 161)
Russian Cooked Cucumbers (pg. 162)
Syrian-Style Okra with Dried Fruit (pg. 168)

SOUPS

Cold Cherry Soup (pg. 54)
Polish Plum and Rhubarb Soup (pg. 61)
Romanian Kohlrabi Soup (pg. 63)
Russian Cold Borscht (pg. 65)
Ruth's Eggless Kneidlach (pg. 67)
Vegetable Broth (pg. 70)
Vegetable Soup (pg. 71)

DESSERTS

Baked Fruit (pg. 174)
Fruit Compote (pg. 175)
Russian Fruit Pudding (pg. 183)

BEVERAGES

Lemonade (pg. 189)
Mint Tea (pg. 190)

DID YOU KNOW...

Yeminite Jews use lemon and salt to pickle, not vinegar. They also use cumin and turmeric with tomato paste, not basil or oregano.

Yeminite Jews use the following condiments with their meals:
Zhoug -- consists primarily of ground green chili peppers and fresh parsley and coriander.
Shatta -- consists primarily of ground red chili peppers and fresh parsley and coriander.
Heilbe -- consists primarily of ground cardamon.

Jews from Iraq break the Yom Kippur fast with almond milk.

The ten most common spices used by Moroccan Jews are cinnamon, cumin, saffron, turmeric, ginger, pepper, cayenne, paprika, aniseed, and sesame seeds.

The seven most common herbs used by Moroccan Jews are onions, garlic, parsley, coriander, basil, marjoram, and mint. Moroccan Jews never use garlic and onion in the same dish.

Twice-fried Russian blinchiki are thin crepe-like white flour pancakes fried on one side then topped and rolled with a filling and baked until crisp. This is the ancestor of the Jewish blintz brought to the United States by Jews from the Ukraine.

Sephardic North African Jews use a lot of cumin, ginger, coriander, cumin, and mint. Vegetables are served with tomato sauce, and desserts are nut-based and use little dairy.

The main grains eaten by East European Ashkenazi Jews are kasha, millet, farina, and wheat. While Georgian and Azerbaijani Jews from Russia eat rice, corn, kasha, and wheat, and Bukharan or central Asian Jews eat rice, kasha, and wheat.

The most common produce eaten by East European Ashkenazi Jews are beets, cabbage, dried prunes, and carrots. Georgian and Azerbaijani Jews from Russia primarily eat eggplant, pomegranate, citrus fruits, grapes, and apricots. Bukharan or central Asian Jews consume pumpkin, carrots, watermelon, pomegranate, and grapes.

Ashkenazi Jews use smaller amounts of herbs and seasonings than do Sephardic Jews.

Fewer than 8,000 Jews are left in India and most of them live in the Bombay area.

There are 40,000 Jews living in Mexico and most of them live in Mexico City. Of these Jews, only 35% are Sephardic.

Half the Jewish population in South America lives in Argentina, primarily in Buenos Aires. The first Jewish community in Argentina started in 1862 in Buenos Aires. Only 18% are Sephardic.

Italian Jewry is the oldest community of the European Diaspora. Its origin goes back to 139 BCE to the Roman Republic.

Jews living in Brighton Beach, New York, today are mainly from the Ukranian City of Odessa.

BIBLIOGRAPHY

The following books and magazines are suggested for those who are interested in learning more about the healthy foods Jews have eaten throughout history. I have also included materials that describe Jews of different backgrounds in an historical context. The travel books are for individuals who would like to visit Jewish neighborhoods throughout the world to learn more about the various cultures and eating habits. Finally, I have listed two books that specifically discuss the topic of Judaism and vegetarianism.

Many of these books and magazines do not have a vegetarian slant. However, all the resources will help the reader gain a better understanding of how Jews have lived through-out history in different parts of the world. The food books I have selected have a healthier slant than other Jewish cookbooks on the marketplace. However, not all the recipes in each cookbook are vegetarian, nor are they all lowfat.

FOOD

The Classic Cuisine of the Italian Jews. By Edda Servi Machlin. Everest House, 1981.

Cookbook for Health (Yiddish). By Lena Brown. Jankovitz, 1931.

Cookbook of the Jews of Greece. By Nicholas Stavroulakis. Lycabettus Press, 1986.

Faye Levy's International Jewish Cookbook. By Faye Levy. Warner Books, 1991.

Food Traditions of Jews from the Soviet Union. By Marion Sitomer. Federation of Jewish Philanthropies, 1982.

Jewish Cooking from Around the World. By Josephine Levy Bacon. Barron's, 1986.

Jewish Manual. By Lady Judith Montefiore. T. and W. Boone, 1846.

Jewish Vegetarian Cooking. By Rose Friedman. Thorsons, 1992.

The Jews of Poland: Recollections and Recipes. By Edouard de Pomiane. Pholiota Press, 1985.

No Cholesterol Passover Recipes. By Charles Stahler and Debra Wasserman. The Vegetarian Resource Group, 1986.

Secrets of a Jewish Baker. By George Greenstein. The Crossing Press, 1993.

The Yeminite Cookbook. By Zion Levi and Hani Agabria. H. Holt, 1988.

HISTORY

Atlas of the Jewish World. By Nicholas de Lange. Facts on File, Inc., 1984.

Bulgaria and Her Jews. By Vicki Tamir. Yeshiva University Press, 1979.

Ethnic America. By Thomas Sowell. Basic Books, Inc., 1981 (Chapter 4).

A History of the Jews in North Africa, Volume I. By H.Z. Hirschberg. E.J. Brill, 1974.

A History of the Jews of Arabia. By Gordon Darnell Newby. University of South Carolina Press, 1988.

The History of the Jews of Italy. By Cecil Roth. Jewish Publication Society of America, 1946.

The Jewish Americans. By Howard Muggamin. Chelsea House Publishers, 1988.

Jewish Life in South America. By J.X. Cohen. Bloch Publishing Company, 1941.

Jewish Societies in the Middle East. Edited by Shlomo Deshen and Walter P. Zenner. University Press of America, Inc., 1982.

Jews in Old China. By Hyman Kublin. Paragon Book Reprint Corporation, 1971.

Jews in Old China. By Sidney Shapiro. Hippocrene Books, 1984.

Jews in Remote Corners of the World. By Ida Cowen. Prentice-Hall, Inc., 1971.

The Jews of Ancient Rome. By Harry J. Leon. The Jewish Publication Society of America, 1960.

The Jews of Arab Lands. By Norman A. Stillman. The Jewish Publication Society of America, 1979.

The Jews of East Central Europe Between The World Wars. By Ezra Mendelsohn. Indiana University Press, 1983.

The Jews of Georgian England (1714-1830). By Todd M. Endelman. The Jewish Publication Society of America, 1979.

The Jews of the Middle East (1860-1972). By Hayyim J. Cohen. John Wiley and Sons, 1973.

The Jews of Spain. By Jane S. Gerber. The Free Press, 1992.

The Jews of Vienna. By Marsha L. Rozenblitt. State University of New York Press, 1983.

The Jews of Yugoslavia. By Harriet Pass Friedenreich. The Jewish Publication Society of America, 1979.

The Legacy of Polish Jewry (1919-1939). By Harry M. Rabinowicz. A.S. Barnes and Company, Inc., 1965.

Mandarins, Jews, and Missionaries. By Michael Pollak. The Jewish Publication Society of America, 1980.

The Other Jews. By Daniel J. Elazar. Basic Books, Inc., 1989.

Poland's Jewish Heritage. By Joram Kagan. Hippocrene Books, 1992.

Russian Jewry (1860-1917). Edited by Jacob Frumkin, Gregor Aronson, and Alexis Goldenweiser. A.S. Barnes and Company, Inc., 1966.

Studies of the Chinese Jews. By Hyman Kublin. Paragon Book Reprint Corporation, 1971.

Vienna and the Jews. By Steven Beller. Cambridge University Press, 1989.

JEWISH MAGAZINES/NEWSLETTERS

Jewish Monthly. By B'nai B'rith International.

The Jewish Vegetarian. By The Jewish Vegetarian and Ecological Society.

Jewish Vegetarians of North America Newsletter. By Jewish Vegetarians of North America.

Kashrus Magazine. By Yeshiva Birkas Reuven.

JUDAISM AND VEGETARIANISM

Judaism and Vegetarianism. By Richard Schwartz. Micah Publications, 1988.

Vegetarianism and Jewish Tradition. By Louis Berman. Ktav, 1981.

TRAVEL

Guide to Jewish Europe. By Asher Israelowitz. The Talman Company, 1988.

Jewish Heritage Travel. By Ruth Ellen Gruber. John Wiley and Sons, Inc., 1992.

Jewish Spain -- A Guide. By Manuel Aguilar and Ian Robertson. Altalena Editores, 1984.

The Jewish Traveler. Edited by Alan M. Tigay. Doubleday and Company, Inc., 1987.

A Travel Guide to Jewish Europe. By Ben G. Frank. Pelican Publishing Company, 1992.

World Guide for the Jewish Traveler. By Warren Freedman. E.P. Dutton, Inc., 1987.

RESOURCES FROM THE VEGETARIAN RESOURCE GROUP

If you are interested in purchasing any of the following VRG titles, please send a check or money order made out to *The Vegetarian Resource Group*, (Maryland residents must add 5% sales tax) and mail it along with your order to: *The Vegetarian Resource Group, P.O. Box 1463, Baltimore, MD 21203*. Make sure you include your shipping address. Or call (410) 366-VEGE to order with a Visa or Mastercard credit card. Price given includes postage in the United States. Outside the USA please pay in US funds by credit card or money order and add $2.00 per book for postage.

MEATLESS MEALS FOR WORKING PEOPLE
Quick and Easy
Vegetarian Recipes
By Debra Wasserman
& Charles Stahler

Vegetarian cooking can be simple or complicated. *The Vegetarian Resource Group* recommends using whole grains and fresh vegetables whenever possible. However, for the busy working person, this isn't always possible.

Meatless Meals For Working People contains over 100 delicious fast and easy recipes, plus ideas which teach you how to be a vegetarian within your hectic schedule using common convenient vegetarian foods. This handy guide also contains a spice chart, party ideas, information on fast food chains, and much, much more.

TRADE PAPERBACK, $6

SIMPLY VEGAN

Quick Vegetarian Meals
By Debra Wasserman
Reed Mangels, Ph.D., R.D.

Simply Vegan is an easy-to-use vegetarian guide that contains over 160 kitchen-tested vegan recipes (no meat, fish, fowl, dairy, or eggs). Each recipe is accompanied by a nutritional analysis.

Reed Mangels, Ph.D., R.D., has included an extensive vegan nutrition section on topics such as Protein, Fat, Calcium, Iron, Vitamin B12, Pregnancy and the Vegan Diet, Feeding Vegan Children, and Calories, Weight Gain, and Weight Loss. A Nutrition Glossary is provided, along with sample menus, meal plans, and a list of the top recipes for iron, calcium, and Vitamin C.

Also featured are food definitions and origins, and a comprehensive list of mail-order companies that specialize in selling vegan food, natural clothing, cruelty-free cosmetics, and ecologically-based household products.

TRADE PAPERBACK $12

NO CHOLESTEROL PASSOVER RECIPES

100 Vegetarian Recipes
By Debra Wasserman
& Charles Stahler

For many, low-calorie Passover recipes are quite a challenge. Here is a wonderful collection of Passover dishes that are non-dairy, no-cholesterol, eggless, and vegetarian. It includes recipes for eggless blintzes, dairyless carrot cream soup, festive macaroons, apple latkes, sweet and sour cabbage, knishes, broccoli with almond sauce, mock "chopped liver," no oil lemon dressing, eggless matzo meal pancakes, and much more.

PAPERBACK $5

VEGETARIAN QUANTITY RECIPES

From The Vegetarian Resource Group

Here is a helpful kit for people who must cook for large groups and institutional settings. It contains 28 vegetarian recipes including main dishes, burgers, sandwich spreads, side dishes, soups, salads, desserts, and breakfast. Each recipe provides a serving for 25 and 50 people, and a nutritional analysis. The kit also contains a listing of companies offering vegetarian food items in institutional sizes and "Tips for Introducing Vegetarian Food Into Institutions." PACKET $15

VEGETARIAN JOURNAL'S FOOD SERVICE UPDATE NEWSLETTER

Edited by The Vegetarian Resource Group staff

This three times a year newsletter is for food service personnel and others working for healthier food in schools, restaurants, hospitals, and other institutions. Vegetarian Journal's Food Service Update offers advice, shares quantity recipes, and spotlights leaders in the industry who are providing the healthy options being looked for by consumers. NEWSLETTER $25 includes both *Vegetarian Journal* and *Vegetarian Journal's FoodService Update*

VEGETARIAN JOURNAL'S GUIDE TO NATURAL FOODS RESTAURANTS IN THE U.S. & CANADA

OVER 2,000 LISTINGS OF RESTAURANTS & VACATION SPOTS

For the health-conscious traveler, this is the perfect traveling companion to insure a great meal or the ideal lodgings when away from home or if you are looking for a nearby vegetarian place.

There has been a delightful proliferation of restaurants designed to meet the growing demand for healthier meals. To help locate these places, there is now a single source for information on over 2,000 restaurants, vacation resorts, and more.

The Vegetarian Journal's Guide to Natural Foods Restaurants (Avery Publishing Group, Inc.) is a helpful guide listing eateries state by state and province by province. Each entry not only describes the house specialties, varieties of cuisine, and special dietary menus, but also includes information on ambiance, attire, and reservations. It even tells you whether or not you can pay by credit card. And there's more. Included in this guide are listings of vegetarian inns, spas, camps, tours, travel agencies, and vacations spots. **Paperback $13**

THE VEGETARIAN GAME

This computer software educational game contains 750 questions. Learn while having fun. Categories include health/nutrition, how food choices affect the environment, animals and ethical choices, vegetarian foods, famous vegetarians, and potluck.

Three age levels: 5-9; 10 or older/adults new to vegetarianism; and individuals with advanced knowledge of vegetarianism or anyone looking for a challenge.

IBM PC compatible with CGA or better or Hercules graphics; MS DOS 2.0 or higher

SOFTWARE $20
When ordering, indicate 3.5" or 5.25" disk.

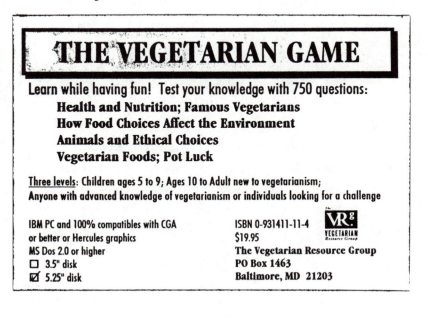

VEGETARIAN JOURNAL REPORTS
Edited by Debra Wasserman & Charles Stahler

This 112-page book consists of the best articles from previous *Vegetarian Journals*. Included are a 28-Day Meal Plan, a Vegetarian Weight Loss Guide, Tips for Changing Your Diet, a Vegetarian Guide for Athletes, Information for Diabetic Diets, plus Indian Recipes, Eggless Dishes, and many more vegetarian resources. PAPERBACK $12

SIMPLE, LOWFAT & VEGETARIAN
By Suzanne Havala, M.S., R.D. and Mary Clifford, R.D.

This 368-page book is an easy-to-use guide to lowfat eating that shows you how to reduce the fat in your meals with a few simple changes, but allows you to continue enjoying dining in Chinese, Mexican, fast food, Indian, natural foods, and other restaurants. You'll also learn what to order when flying, traveling on Amtrak, going to the movies, or visiting an amusement park. Good food choices, before and after menu magic, fat content of foods, and helpful charts are presented for these and many other situations. The book also contains 30 days of quick lowfat meals, tips on how to modify your own recipes, sample menus, weekly shopping lists, plus 50 vegan recipes. PAPERBACK $15

SUBSCRIBE TO
VEGETARIAN JOURNAL

The practical magazine for those interested in health, ecology, and ethics.

Each issue features:

- **Nutrition Hotline** -- answers your questions about vegetarian diets.
- **Low-fat Vegetarian Recipes** --- quick and easy dishes, international cuisine, and gourmet meals.
- **Natural Food Product Reviews**
- **Scientific Updates** -- a look at recent scientific papers relating to vegetarianism.
- **Vegetarian Action** -- projects by individuals and groups.

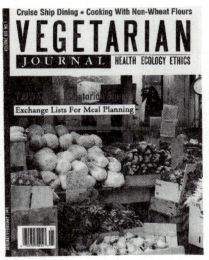

VEGETARIAN Journal ISSN 0885-7636 is published bi-monthly by the independent Vegetarian Resource Group.

To receive a one year subscription, send a check for $20.00 to The Vegetarian Resource Group, PO Box 1463, Baltimore, MD 21203. Canadian and Mexican subscriptions are $30.00 per year and other foreign country subscriptions are $40 per year. All non USA subscriptions must be paid in U.S. funds by postal order or Mastercard/Visa credit card.

Name: _____

Address: _____

_____ Zip: _____

WHAT IS THE VEGETARIAN RESOURCE GROUP?

Our health professionals, activists, and educators work with businesses and individuals to bring about healthy changes in your school, workplace, and community. Registered dietitians and physicians aid in the development of practical nutrition related publications and answer member or media questions about the vegetarian diet.

Vegetarian Journal **is one of the benefits members enjoy.** Readers receive practical tips for vegetarian meal planning, articles on vegetarian nutrition, recipes, natural food product reviews, and an opportunity to share ideas with others. All nutrition articles are reviewed by a registered dietitian or medical doctor.

The Vegetarian Resource Group also publishes books and special interest newsletters such as *Vegetarian Journal's Food Service Update* and *Tips for Vegetarian Activists*.

The Vegetarian Resource Group is a non-profit organization. Financial support comes primarily from memberships, contributions and book sales. **Membership includes the bimonthly** *Vegetarian Journal*. To join, send $20 to The Vegetarian Resource Group, P.O. Box 1463, Baltimore, Maryland 21203.

INDEX

To order additional copies of
THE LOWFAT
JEWISH VEGETARIAN COOKBOOK,
send $15 per book to The Vegetarian Resource Group,
PO Box 1463, Baltimore, MD 21203.

To Join
The Vegetarian Resource Group
and Receive the Bimonthly
Vegetarian Journal
for One Year
Send $20.00 to The Vegetarian Resource Group,
P.O. Box 1463,
Baltimore, MD 21203.